THE OVERTHINKING CHRONICLES

CULTIVATING YOUR INNER COMEDIAN TO
REFRAME ANXIETY, SPARK SELF-COMPASSION &
TRUST, AND GIVE SELF-DOUBT THE PUNCHLINE
IT DESERVES

SARCRASSTIC SELF CARE

SARA TONINSTAN

MOD COUPLE

MCP

PUBLISHING

The Overthinking Chronicles

Cultivating Your Inner Comedian to Reframe Anxiety, Spark Self-Compassion and Trust, and Give Self-Doubt the Punchline It Deserves

PRAISE FOR SARA TONINSTAN

"The Overthinking Chronicles is a humorous and insightful journey into the world of overthinking and anxiety, offering a refreshing perspective on overcoming these challenges. Through relatable storytelling and practical advice, this book covers a wide range of topics, from the science behind laughter to the benefits of self-deprecating humor and the importance of support systems. Irreverent, entertaining and ND-friendly, Toninstan's candid writing style makes this book a valuable resource for anyone looking to break the cycle of overthinking and embrace a more light-hearted approach to life." —Catherine Smith, PsyD
Licensed Psychologist

"For the overthinkers and ND humans of the world, this book is a must-read. One of those books you can't put down, Toninstan's writing is witty, and the personal storytelling woven into the fabric of this book will have you belly laughing one moment and pensive the next. It is deeply honest, sincere, and paints a realistic picture of what it is like to be an overthinker. The science-backed information shared and practical, snack-sized tips are easy to digest and implement. The perspective of using self-deprecating humor for your well-being is a fresh and novel one. With a candid and real delivery, you feel like you're sitting next to a best friend chatting about how you overthink overthinking."
—Karrie Lemansky Straub
ADHD Coach & Business Mentor

"The Overthinking Chronicles is a delightful convergence where science meets sass to help you kick anxiety's ass to achieve mental peace and bring more positivity to your life! Toninstan provides practical, playful, and easy to implement strategies for the lifelong 'professional' overthinker who has been searching for effective ways to be more compassionate with themselves, and learn how to make different choices to improve their wellbeing. Every story shared is a great reminder that so often we think we need complex solutions to our persistent problems, but Sara demonstrates in her straightforward and uniquely enlightening book that simple IS significant AND sufficient. At the heart of our diversity lies a singular truth. We are all human, and by purposely infusing more humor into your life, you can live within uncertainty with much more grace and joy. This book is the radically different approach to a universally human experience that we've been needing in these modern and absurd times." —Sharon Calderón

Certified Life Coach, Play Educator, & Activist

ACKNOWLEDGMENTS

SO MANY PEOPLE HELPED MAKE THIS BOOK POSSIBLE—TOO MANY
TO NAME, REALLY. I AM GRATEFUL TO MY FAMILY, AND ESPECIALLY
MY PARTNER WHO ALWAYS ENCOURAGES ME AND ENTHUSIASTICALLY
SUPPORTS EVERY DECISION I MAKE. I SHOULD THANK MY KIDS AS
WELL FOR DEALING WITH THEIR "BAT-SHIT CRAZY"
NEURODIVERGENT MOM, WHO ONLY RECENTLY DISCOVERED SHE HAS
ADHD. (BUT IN THE END, I GUESS *THEY* CAN THANK *ME* FOR
PASSING DOWN THAT GIFT TO THEM. AREN'T GENETICS FUN?)

I AM GRATEFUL TO MY FRIENDS, WHO, UNBEKNOWNST TO THEM,
HAHA, CONSTITUTE THE VERY FABRIC OF THIS BOOK IN THE ABSURD
STORIES THAT I HAVE THE PRIVILEGE OF RETELLING AND REFRAMING
FOR THIS CONTEXT IN HOPES THAT MY CHAOTIC BRAIN WILL MAKE
OTHERS FEEL SEEN AND LESS ALONE. AND I AM GRATEFUL TO ALL
THE EARLY READERS WHO GENEROUSLY GAVE THEIR TIME AND
FEEDBACK TO HELP ME MAKE THIS BOOK THE BEST IT CAN BE.

I AM ALSO THANKFUL FOR MY PARENTS AND SIBLINGS, WHO HAVE
SUPPORTED ME MY ENTIRE LIFE. EVEN IF THEY THOUGHT SOME OF
MY PATHS WERE CRAZY, THEY ALWAYS ACCEPTED ME FOR WHO I AM.
MY PARENTS ALWAYS LET ME BE ME.

I WISH MY PARENTS WERE STILL ALIVE TO WITNESS THIS MOMENT. I KNOW THEY'D BE PROUD. MY MOM WOULD BE UTTERLY THRILLED AND PROBABLY GUSH AND BRAG ABOUT ME TO HER FRIENDS, AND MY DAD — THOUGH HE'D SIGH AT ALL THE CUSS WORDS — WOULD ALSO BE GENUINELY HAPPY FOR ME. MY PARENTS RAISED ME TO TRUST MYSELF AND FOLLOW MY DREAMS. THEY DIDN'T WANT ME TO FEAR CHASING PASSION OVER PRAGMATISM (THOUGH MY DAD DID ALWAYS SAY THAT HAVING A PLAN B WAS NEVER A BAD IDEA), AND THAT IS A PERSPECTIVE OF PRIVILEGE THAT IS NOT LOST ON ME.

IN THE END, I'M GONNA PULL A SNOOP DOG AND SAY "I WANNA THANK ME," 'CAUSE YEAH, I'D LIKE TO THANK ME FOR BELIEVING IN ME AND FOR DOING ALL THIS HARD WORK, AND I'D LIKE TO THANK ME FOR NEVER QUITTING.
EXCEPT WHEN IT COMES TO OVERTHINKING.

*To all the beautiful misfits, anxious mavericks &
neurodivergent, overthinking weirdo punks.
Thank you. I see you,
and the world needs you.*

CONTENTS

ACRONYMS & ABBREVIATIONS USED IN THIS BOOK... WAY MORE THAN I REALIZED...

- ADD Anxiety and Depression Disorder (also Attention Deficit Disorder, as ADHD was formerly called)
- ADHD Attention Deficit Hyperactivity Disorder
- AFAB Assigned Female At Birth
- AI Artificial Intelligence (ChatGPT, Alexa, etc.)
- AKA Also Known As
- AMAB Assigned Male At Birth
- ASD Autism Spectrum Disorder
- AuDHD Used to describe an Autistic person who has ADHD
- BD Bipolar Disorder
- BO Body Odor
- CSI Crime Scene Investigation
- GAD Generalized Anxiety Disorder
- IBS Irritable Bowel Syndrome
- ND Neurodivergent
- NT Neurotypical
- OCD Obsessive-Compulsive Disorder
- PBR Pabst Blue Ribbon, a very cheap American beer

- PD Panic Disorder
- Pepto: Short for Pepto Bismol, an over-the-counter medicine that provides relief from nausea, diarrhea and upset stomach
- RBF an inherently sexist term that stands for Resting Bitch Face & is more commonly directed toward women who don't smile as men would like them to even though they are not upset or annoyed.
- Rom-Com: Romantic Comedy
- SCTV Second City Television, a Canadian sketch comedy show that ran from 1976-84
- SNL Saturday Night Live, an American sketch comedy show on the air since 1975
- SSRI Selective Serotonin Reuptake Inhibitor or Serotonin-Specific Reuptake Inhibitor
- TMZ an American celebrity news website whose name stands for Thirty-Mile Zone, the historic studio intersection of West Beverly Boulevard and North La Cienega Boulevard in Los Angeles, California.
- TP Toilet Paper (in the US, but the Brits commonly refer to toilet tissue as loo rolls. I don't think there's an LR abbreviation in this book:)
- VA Virtual Assistant

PROLOGUE

MY DEAR FELLOW OVERTHINKERS,

WELCOME TO *THE OVERTHINKING CHRONICLES!*

Sara Toninstan here, and I will be your faithful guide on this self-care odyssey. Although I have succeeded at failing as a professional musician, a waitress, and a wife, among so many other things in life, my failure to be happy as a tenured college professor may be my most tremendous success to date.

Yep! I finally stopped overthinking my profound exhaustion, growing apathy, and ultimate lack of creative and financial fulfillment and left the "security" of my job that boasted annual increases in health insurance premiums, an email inbox with 10,000 unread messages, and a monthly paycheck whose net had not increased in ten years. With 37 articles in varied degrees of completion lying around my office at any given moment, I mastered the art of overthinking and underachieving and even dabbled in a bit of self-sabotage. And yet, despite the chaos in my mind, I always managed to find time to tidy up my office and make it look like I had it all together. By leaving that job and essentially abandoning a career I had spent years and years of schooling to prepare for (not to mention a subsequent ADHD diagnosis, and hey, let's throw enduring menopause in there, too, to make it extra fun), I have learned to embrace my neurodivergent quirks and use them as catalysts for creative fulfillment and joy, with the bonus of zero adjustments to being broke!

Always the "class clown," I am now determined to help others declutter the $h*t out of their overthinking, anxious minds through self-compassion and humor. The point being, after years of overthinking this book, my ever-sardonic self finally said "f*ck it" and decided to publish it, much to the chagrin of the perfectionist voices in my head that have been sabotaging my dreams through fear since forever.

This book provides unconventional, humorous ways to *manage* anxiety. It combines self-deprecating and self-compassionate strategies to build confidence and trust. It is ideal for those who feel overwhelmed by the cycle of anxious thoughts and want to find some inner peace via humor. As I'll detail more at the end of the introduction, I hope you will learn to reframe negative thoughts, understand why you feel the way you do, and frankly laugh at yourself a little more.

But let's get down to brass tacks: firstly, this book is *not* a substitute for medical treatment, therapy, or mental health care. I have based this book on my lived experience as someone who is late-diagnosed ADHD, has two AuDHD kids (plus a bonus OCD diagnosis for one of the kids), has struggled with mental health throughout my life, and learned to manage it through years of therapy, learned coping mechanisms through treatment and beyond, and yes, medication, so its primary purposes are to entertain, inspire, motivate, and help you feel less alone.

Secondly, if you are looking for a redundant, traditional bullshit way of getting rid of anxious thoughts, this book is not for you. And finally, notice that I did not censor the "shit" part of the word "bullshit" as I did with my previous cuss words. That said, please note: I also swear. A lot in real life. It's who I am; I understand I am not for everyone. That said, I've reined it in slightly in this book, for sure, but if you are offended by the word "shit," or heaven help us all [gasp], the occasional F-bomb, then this book may not be for you.

Or maybe, *just maybe*, this book IS for you: if you give my trash mouth half a chance, you might admit that even if you don't swear in front of others, you know you've belted out a DAMMIT (or worse) at least once in your life and felt the sweet relief of that release. If you want to approach over-thinking humorously, which is probably the best approach to many things in life, then you are my people. Read on!

While our minds work in our favor, they can sometimes do the opposite, and I have decided to leverage the wild, erratic behavior that my brain can produce. I am sure over-thinking has conjured up all kinds of absurd scenarios for you as it has for me, so why can't we make fun of it with self-deprecating humor and an occasional sprinkle of optimistic sarcasm? I will, if you will.

Now let's go!

Love,

Sara

INTRODUCTION

NEVER HAVE I EVER...

"Overthinking is like being trapped in a haunted house of your own making, where the ghosts are just your thoughts, and they won't stop laughing at your misery." — Unknown

Have you ever spent a night in bed lying wide awake trying to evaluate something silly from eight years ago, like when you got really drunk and lost your phone, wallet, and dignity but never left the house? Maybe you missed brunch with friends earlier in the day and wonder if they think you are a total asshole now? Or you think your boss is annoyed with you for microwaving fish in the office kitchen.

Whatever the reason keeping you up at night, it's causing you to overthink. It's giving you insomnia, and all this hyper-fixation can feel like life is one constant shit-storm. Some people will just tell us to "get over it," which, BTW, is the worst advice ever, but the reality is that regardless of your diagnosis (or lack thereof) of ADHD, ASD, OCD, BD, PD, GAD, etc., for all of us overthinkers, it's not that simple. It's a complex issue characterized by various factors such as anxiety, depression, perfectionism, low self-esteem, past traumas, and personality traits. With the addition of bad habits, overthinking can be reinforced and lead to dwelling on negative thoughts or, worse, catastrophizing (assuming the worst scenario in any or every situation, like thinking you might get trapped in an elevator or attacked by an army of rabid zombie pigeons during a morning stroll).

There are certainly some perks to overthinking. I mean, look at Albert Einstein, who pretty much made a career from it. Still, when you get suffocated and overwhelmed by a perpetual cycle of overthinking, you need to consider finding a way to switch off your overactive tornado brain. When negative thoughts and memories flood your mind, you can ponder and dwell and deliberate and analyze for hours upon days, soon locking yourself in not only a mental prison but a pseudo-physical one, too, ultimately preventing you from enjoying the life you deserve to have. We are all guilty of overthinking at some point, and that is okay. Who hasn't cringed and then shrieked at a badly aged Facebook post from ten years ago about literally anything? Who knows? In another ten years, you can look back on today and not stress about the social media posts … because they won't exist because you were too terrified to post anything anyway. I remember when I could barely take a selfie, and sometimes I wonder: if hell exists, is it full of every deleted selfie, every reel left in the purgatory of Instagram and TikTok drafts? Now, that is terrifying.

As an overthinker, you're probably terrified of many things. How about a game of "Never Have I Ever" based on chronic overthinking? You might not know the rules if you have never had a sleepover or your parents never forced you to go to summer camp. It's relatively simple: players take turns listing experiences they never had, and anyone who has must take a drink (in summer camp and sleepovers, it was juice, I promise). We can replace a drink for each statement you can relate to with a deep breath instead. Or scream into a pillow. They'll both do fine.

So, as an overthinker, never have I ever:

• Felt a lack of confidence and low self-esteem due to feeling overwhelmed by anxious thoughts. We might try to hide this with humor, but in reality, we feel completely stuck.

Example: It was prom night, back in the days before social media. I picked up my date (yes, really; he was a friend and didn't have his driver's license yet). We had a photo taken, but behind my frozen smile, I was paranoid that everyone looked better than me, danced better than me, or maybe I would win something and get covered in pig blood like in the horror movie *Carrie*. I couldn't stop overthinking and never enjoyed the night as I should have.

• Felt like nobody else could relate to being overwhelmed with overthinking. If it weren't already embarrassing or shameful enough, connecting with others on a deep emotional level is way more challenging when you believe no one understands you.

Example: In my early years in academia as a junior faculty member at the university, where I worked for 17 years, I felt immense pressure to get tenure. I accepted every opportunity, seeking approval from my department chair and the Dean. Consequently, I spent more time with students and colleagues than with my family early on. I felt I was neglecting my (now ex) husband and children while feeling that, ironically, my colleagues didn't even know the real me. The workload was unmanageable for me and caused my stress levels to soar. Fearful of appearing incompetent, I kept quiet and pushed myself to burnout. Even after earning tenure, imposter syndrome and overthinking persisted, and I questioned whether I deserved it. Throughout this pursuit of professional validation, I sacrificed quality time with my family. I struggled to find balance, plagued by lingering doubt and insecurity that I didn't feel like I could share with anyone.

• Felt powerless and hopeless due to overwhelming feelings derived from overthinking, AKA analysis paralysis.

Example: Many moons ago, I contemplated enrolling in a ballroom dancing class. My friend Janet always invited me out to Salsa dancing, and overthinking perfectionist that I was, I hated that I didn't know how to dance like a pro. Despite being a skilled musician and having reached the *pointe* level in ballet as a child, my overthinking nature made me highly anxious about joining the class. On top of this, since my husband at the time wouldn't do it with me, I'd have to dance with strangers, intensifying my self-doubt. Despite my good rhythm, I couldn't shake the fear of looking clumsy or not getting the moves immediately. When the time came to sign up, I found myself paralyzed by overthinking. What if I constantly step on my partner's toes? What if I accidentally spin too fast and lose my balance? What if I can't deal with the gendered nature of traditional partnered dancing and keep wanting to lead? What if my nervousness makes me sweat profusely, and my dance partner gags from my nasty BO?

In the end, I abandoned the idea of joining the class altogether, feeling hopeless about my prospects of being able to perform a badass scene from *Dirty Dancing* [insert your fave iconic dance film here...I'm partial to *Saturday Night Fever*, but if you're more a *Breakin' 2: Electric Boogaloo*, *Flashdance*, or *Footloose* type, you do you!] the next time I went out. As much as I had wanted to learn Swing and Salsa dancing, I had convinced myself that I couldn't do it, and instead of having fun when I went out dancing with Janet, I felt overwhelmed. The only exercise I got was the endless overthinking that occupied my mind.

• Had trouble trusting your judgment, so much that taking risks or making decisions was difficult. This difficulty may also relate to feeling inferior and believing others know better than you. (We're looking at you, Imposter Syndrome!)

Example: My best friend Tracy's birthday was coming up, and a surprise party was planned. My other friends asked me for ideas about how they could help. Of course, I knew what she would love: "a pub crawl in London" theme would be ideal, with lots of bougie beer flights. Or a French cheese-tasting tour with stinky-ass goats' milk cheeses. But then I thought, "What if I'm wrong?" I couldn't handle the thought of messing up such a big event, so I reluctantly ushered someone else to take the reins. And guess what? It was shit. Think PBR and American "cheese" singles wrapped in plastic. Okay, not that shitty, but you get my point. I should have trusted my gut, but I had to pretend to get low-key buzzed on beer so cheap that even my teenage self would have scoffed.

• Felt stuck in a mundane routine that doesn't fulfill you. Even though you know what you should do, you are too anxious to do anything about it. (There's that damn analysis paralysis again.)

Example: At one point in my life, whenever I got home from work, I would cherish my little downtime. I mistakenly even thought I should continue to work by grading papers and answering student emails. But while there were a million side projects I wanted to tackle, I often ended up perched on the couch watching Netflix. Why? Because to start something, anything, was too giant a leap of faith. Instead, this mundane routine of watching crap after crap made me feel worse and worse. Meanwhile, I should have been working on something more productive and meaningful. Or, better yet, just relaxing.

Okay, wow! Hopefully, by now, you're feeling less alone and calmer from all those deep breaths you just took instead of drinks, or perhaps you've destroyed a pillow. People often shrug away the thought of overthinking, but not addressing this influx of hyper-fixations can severely impact our health. Recent studies have revealed that negative or intrusive thoughts harm our mental and physical health. Such thoughts are associated with higher levels of inflammation in the body, which can cause our overall physical health to deteriorate (James et al., 2023).

Before today's technological insurgence, anxiety was not nearly as pronounced or acknowledged, and Adult ADHD and in women in particular? Forget about it! Anxious people spent their time fake smiling by day and crying in the shower by night. I know I did. However, with therapy becoming less stigmatized and more encouraged and the marvelous invention of the Internet, we can now quickly access previously unavailable knowledge. We know now that not only is anxiety in its countless incarnations and manifestations a severe issue, but it's also possible to quell it with a little or a lot of humor in addition to medication and therapy, should you need those.

When I used to overthink and then FINALLY acknowledged it, I sought out effective strategies to overcome it. Some made sense, others did not, and more than once, I fell down some online rabbit holes and impulsively paid money for products that promised quick fixes for my problems. (I'm looking at you, focus apps!) I had to have an honest talk with myself. "Do I want to start enjoying my life more and worry less, or am I just going to convince myself for the 100th time that I don't need to do anything about this debilitating over-thinking?"

At this point, you might be wondering, who am I to tell you about anxiety and overthinking? Maybe I am some crazy con artist who just busted out of prison and is currently sitting in Starbucks with a stolen MacBook Pro? Well, my MacBook is not stolen, though I may or may not be sitting in Starbucks right now. Okay, the only thing I am crazy about is helping you feel less anxious and less alone. Who better to write a book about overthinking than someone who's lived it for, gulp, over half a century now ... late diagnosed ADHDer here ..., studied it for over 20 years due to my own and kids' diagnoses ... career academic and AuDHD mom here ..., and ultimately learned to manage the crap out of it ... massive therapy and medication fan here ...? I used to have panic attacks from anxiety and things I thought I couldn't change. But guess what? While it's true that there's no cure for ADHD, I *could* change *many* of the things killing me and *manage* my issues with self-knowledge, self-love, and care, and viable strategies that, while they may not work for others, work for me, and that realization gave me strength and purpose.

I have failed in many things, but these failures shaped me and ultimately led to finding the best version of myself. When I left my career as a tenured university professor, I also quit much of the stress and overthinking that came with it. You might think, "But isn't that a great job?" Any job that offers security is on some level, but it wasn't as financially stable for me as you might think. I was so miserable living paycheck to paycheck and working a second job. The point is it was holding me back from unleashing my full potential. I can now utilize my knowledge and experiences to empower others, and if that means helping others get to where I am faster, isn't that a more remarkable success story?

So, please think of me as something between the coolest teacher you ever had and an honest bestie as I navigate you toward outsmarting overthinking, and becoming a master of your destiny. My background in the scholarship of teaching and learning, education, and student mentoring and success has gifted me with many things, from the various types of learning styles to researching case studies to comparing effective strategies and employing best practices to solve problems.

But enough with all the seriousness for a moment. When I started this book, I pictured the younger version of me, who wished she had known the version of me now to help her navigate this chaotic life. As of today, I can confirm that things have gotten so much better, such that the crazy scenarios I used to imagine lost their power. Honestly, the more time and energy we spend focusing on things we can't control, the less control we have over what we actually can control. That's some stoic shit right there. I know I can't go back in time, nor would I want to, because my failures cultivated a mindset of strength and grit. For one, I got married young, though unlike many, I decided after 20+ years of anxiety to unmarry (and hey, I got some awesome kids). Perhaps you think I am on a wild crusade in full mid-life crisis to have left my married life and a job for which I spent ten years toiling away to get a Ph.D. Or, maybe I was finally ready to rip off the masks and live my life the way I always wanted. I just hope anyone reading this can reach their goals slightly faster than I did.

Here's the deal. I want this book to have a positive impact on your life. Let's look at the specific ways it'll make a difference. My ultimate goal is for you to be able to:

- Reframe negative thoughts and look at them from a more balanced perspective or find a way to turn off the endless loop of anxious thoughts altogether;
- Learn how to be kinder and more compassionate towards yourself;
- Make peace with the past, allowing you to move forward without regret or guilt;
- Learn to laugh at yourself without inhibiting your standards or self-worth;
- Understand why you feel the way you do and trust yourself more, and ultimately,
- Manage anxiety better and make decisions with greater confidence.

There are so many books about overthinking and dealing with anxiety, and many offer great tips. I can't say I've read them all, but I have made every effort to extract the valuable stuff and have learned from both the gems and the duds. I researched so much that I finished Google, and ChatGPT is now coming to me for prompts and content.

All joking aside, I was a professor dealing with multiple courses and many different students every semester while publishing all kinds of lofty academic blather and doing conference presentations. So, I am *really good* at conducting and culling through deep research and being resourceful. However, my biggest takeaway from many self-help books was that while they offered many nuanced tips, tricks, and legit therapeutic strategies, *I couldn't seem to relate to them.* Should I pay over $1000 to go on a silent retreat? Would I climb a mountain for four hours to squeeze in ten minutes of meditation? While that might help some (I'm looking at you, neurotypical friends!), it's not for me.

I used humor all the time in my teaching to help students

remember things. When dealing with serious topics or issues, humor can help you digest the information you attain and make it stick. Don't believe me? Wouldn't you remember the funniest ones you ever heard if I asked you to tell me a joke? If I asked for a funny story, would you have one ingrained in your mind? Humor is a powerful tool that we should all use more often. No matter your age, dietary requirements, or star sign, humor can always help alleviate difficult moments in life; for example, have you ever heard the best man speech at a wedding? Standing in front of a big crowd and giving an emotionally driven speech about your best friend that's deeper than a Chicago-style pizza pan can be daunting. But sprinkling a dash of humor on it guarantees it will be memorable years from now.

I experienced this firsthand recently when I delivered the eulogy at my dad's funeral. Okay, yeah, sorry to get all sad and morbid on you, but if you're still reading, let's call ourselves friends. The fact is, I spoke for only seven minutes at my dad's funeral, but I sprinkled humor throughout (it wasn't hard: my dad was quietly hilarious). Although it may be counterintuitive to laugh at funerals, the funny stories about my dad had people rolling. I guarantee you, those funny stories helped ease the grief. All these people learned things about my dad that they never knew, and my comedic delivery of those stories will make them unforgettable to all who heard them. Humor is *that* powerful.

The reason I wrote this and why it's different from other overthinking, overthinker "edutainment" lived experience books is that the integration of humor with some legit research at the core makes it more accessible to everyday folks and can help dispel many myths with a laugh without coming off as too technical and science-y. Plus, I'm pretty sure you won't find my awesome word "science-y" in any solid (but not nearly as much fun) anxiety-related books. Bonus! We can tackle intrusive thoughts with an obnoxious cackle and lasso anxiety with a smile (and not the frozen fake kind). Don't get me wrong. You *will* learn. But more importantly, I hope you will laugh.

As you progress through this book, you will experience self-deprecating humor based on my own lived experiences, some of which you, my overthinking siblings in arms, may have encountered as well. *Being able to laugh at ourselves is a gift.* I hope that after you have read this book, the only time you dwell on shit is to make light of it or, better yet, laugh uproariously about it. As a seasoned and recovering over-thinker, I can recall my memories and experiences, but now I stress and worry less, and the life-long old-soul smart-ass in me shrugs them off with a laugh. And you can, too. You can.

So, with some insight, exploration, and acknowledgment, are you ready to face your anxiety head-on and try to unravel the string of chaos that looms in your brain? Let's stop procrastinating due to self-doubt and give overthinking the middle finger once and for all.

CHAPTER ONE

DYING LAUGHING IN THE FACE OF DOOM: HARNESSING HUMOR TO COMBAT THE OVERTHINKING PLAGUE

"WHEN WE REMEMBER we are all mad, the mysteries disappear, and life stands explained." — Mark Twain

You've probably heard the phrase "laughter is the best medicine," but what if there was a lot of truth to it? What if laughter was the key to unlocking a whole range of perks that we never even knew about? What if harnessing humor could radically transform your mental resilience and, ultimately, your mental health?

Nothing can pull you out of a foul mood faster than something hilarious. I mean, who hasn't secretly shared the iconic "distracted boyfriend" or "woman yelling at a cat" memes? There have undoubtedly been countless times when a challenging situation shifted drastically because of humor.

Once, my former colleague Karen (yes, I said Karen. Lots of us Gen Xers are named Karen) was having a frustrating time in a meeting. The conversation was getting heated, so much so that everybody was talking loudly over each other, like some scene from Wall Street at the New York Stock Exchange. Karen was stressed, experiencing some massive

ADHD-style sensory overload, and feeling like she wasn't being heard. Each time she tried to suggest an idea, someone else would interrupt. She couldn't take it anymore and had enough. Karen suddenly stood up and yelled, "You all sound like a bunch of angry Chewbaccas!" Karen's spontaneous remark was initially met with silence, and for a second, she was embarrassed by her outburst. She thought it was bad enough that her name was Karen and certainly did not want to "be one." Suddenly, our friend Pablo laughed, followed by another colleague and another. The tension in the room dissipated as everyone was hysterically laughing. Karen's brutal comment helped everyone step back and approach the conversation in a much better and calmer way, giving her the floor to finally suggest her awesome idea.

For Karen, humor fantastically turned the situation around in her favor. Had she not made a joke, that meeting could have spiraled chaotically, and it would have taken longer for everyone to reach a conclusion. Karen didn't just luck out with her funny comment; humor is incredible for difficult situations. Read that again: it sounds counterintuitive, but it's entirely true. Also note: Karen and her absurd Chewbacca comment are now part of a fucking book. This book. That you're reading right now. Yeah, that's right! Why? It was hilarious, and I will never forget that day thanks to her now iconic, stressed-out "outburst."

Now, I am not considering extreme situations like hostage negotiation or finding your significant other in bed with a Victoria's Secret lingerie-clad model (though anything in this life is possible). But a bit of humor can help shift things in your favor. Ever accidentally fall onto a friend, then both laugh seconds later? I have. Or smile at your Tinder date with spinach stuck in your teeth, only for them to point it out and do the same? (Okay, fine, I have never used Tinder, but I have had plenty of shit stuck in my teeth in public.) Heck, there was even once a contestant on American Idol who farted during her 4th audition and is probably a millionaire now. In a challenging situation, humor, especially self-deprecating humor, can help by:

- **Diffusing tension:** Humor can help diffuse tension in a difficult situation. For example, if two people are arguing, cracking a joke or making a lighthearted comment instead of insulting them will help ease the tension and redirect the conversation to a more productive path.
- **Coping with stress:** Humor can also help people cope with stress. For example, if someone is going through a difficult time, watching a funny movie or reading a humorous book can help take their mind off their problems and provide a much-needed break.
- **Improving communication:** Humor can also improve communication in a difficult situation. For example, if a supervisor needs to give an employee constructive critical feedback, humor can help soften the blow and make the conversation less negative.
- **Finding common ground:** Humor can help people find common ground in difficult situations. For example, if two people have different perspectives on a topic, using humor to highlight the absurdity of both perspectives can help them see the similarities between them and work toward a compromise.

I told my old pal Johnny that I was working on this book. Johnny is hilarious and one of those friends who seems to have a story for everything, so he gave me one. He recalled going for this job "interview" for a lucrative gig during the pandemic, and he confided in me that he was anxious about it, which was a real surprise since he is always so confident. Johnny plays punk music with a traditional Scottish flair, and he explained that many other traditional Irish and Scottish musicians were waiting when he arrived. He thought there was no way he would get this job. Some dressed "better" (those kilts, though!), and some were more conventionally "attractive" (longest beard contestant anyone?!). Some were even lilting loudly on their phones about their gazillion Instagram followers and the hundreds of fans that showed up to their last gig at some iconic pub (probably all fake talking to no one). Johnny's stomach was churning, and his heart was beginning to race. As he entered the room, he sat down, and a receptionist asked his name. Johnny's mind went blank, and though he opened his mouth, the only sound that came out of his body was from his ass. That's right: he farted. Johnny quickly gathered his thoughts, "Oh, thank god I remembered my bagpipes!" Everyone in the room exploded with laughter, followed by a secretly reluctant Johnny, which helped relax him enough to smash the interview and get a call with an offer for the gig.

Now, I am not saying the next time you are in a situation, you should fart. My point is this: Johnny could have left that room after his butt interrupted the interview, but instead, he persevered and prevailed because after laughing, he was calmer and more focused on continuing. Johnny's self-deprecating humor, in particular, really flipped the script. As a result, he could make fun of himself before others might while simultaneously getting them to laugh *with* him rather than *at* him.

A whole bunch of incredible things happen by simply laughing, and did I mention it's free? After laughing, some short-term benefits can include:

- **Stress relief.** Laughing helps activate the body's stress response mechanism, firing it up before cooling it down. In other words, increasing and decreasing your heart rate and blood pressure results in a relaxed feeling.
- **Organ stimulation**. A good chuckle improves your intake of oxygen-rich air, which stimulates the lungs, heart, and muscles. It also helps the brain release endorphins and boosts serotonin, our happy hormones.
- **Tension relief.** Laughing stimulates circulation and helps muscles relax, reducing physical symptoms of stress.
- **Muscle relaxation.** Laughing helps relax your muscles by reducing tension.
- **Pain relief.** As mentioned, laughing triggers the release of endorphins, which help relieve pain.
- **Improved immune function.** Laughter improves immune function by increasing the production of antibodies and activating those cells.
- Amazingly, **it burns calories**. Laughing can help you lose weight—not enough to be Weight Watcher of the Month, but still pretty darn good. One study by researchers at Vanderbilt University Medical School determined that laughing for ten to fifteen minutes burns between ten and forty calories (Buchowski et al., 2005).

It almost sounds like witchcraft, but science can back me up. For a long time, we have known that many activities such as exercise, listening to music, twerking, and massive orgasms help release endorphins. Yet, the power of laughing is still a relatively new area. According to University of Oxford professor Robin Dunbar, researchers need to focus more on why we laugh and its role. Dunbar theorizes that by laughing, the brain unleashes endorphins, the happy hormone responsible for relieving pain and ignoring it, as just mentioned. One study that first explored this concept tested participants for their pain threshold by wrapping one of their arms in a frozen wine-cooling sleeve or blood-pressure cuff until they couldn't take it anymore (although electrode nipple clamps could have sufficed). After the initial non-nipple test, the participants were exposed to either a control or laugh-inducing test; then, their pain levels were tested again. The tests involved watching classic clips from *Friends* and *Mr. Bean* episodes and a live show from the infamous Edinburgh Fringe Festival. The participants were tested alone and in groups, as laughter is thirty times more likely to happen when in a social context. The results showed that participants' pain tolerance jumped after laughing, and on average, after watching fifteen minutes of comedy in a group, the pain threshold increased by ten percent. In contrast, participants tested alone showed smaller increases (Dunbar et al., 2012).

So, why did laughter help these lucky participants? The researchers believe it's due to a long series of exhalations caused by laughing so much, which exhausted the abdominal muscles, triggering the release of endorphins. Yep, your body's natural pain-killing hormone helps produce feelings of pleasure and euphoria and improves your mood. Humor can also trigger these hormones. However, these are not the only hormones greatly affected by humor. We can also benefit from the following:

- **Dopamine:** Your most fun friend. It is a unique neurotransmitter that plays a role in the brain's reward and pleasure centers. Laughter can increase dopamine levels, leading to feelings of happiness, motivation, and pleasure.

- **Serotonin:** Dopamine's loyal bestie. It is a hormone known for sleep but is also associated with mood regulation and appetite. Laughter has also been shown to increase serotonin levels, which can help improve mood, lower stress and anxiety, and promote a feeling of well-being.
- **Cortisol**: Dopamine and Serotonin's arch-nemesis. It is a hormone released as a response to stress. Laughter helps reduce cortisol levels, which in turn helps reduce stress, improve immune function, and increase overall well-being.

Our precious, powerful brains have 86 billion neurons, yet it's believed that we know only ten to fifteen percent of what is going on in there (and as an overthinker, maybe it's best we don't know). We DO, however, know that humor can play a pivotal role, and not only with short-term effects. What if I were to tell you that regular laughter could potentially lower the risk of getting heart disease?

According to a study from the Center for Preventive Cardiology at the University of Maryland Medical Center, laughter is a great way to protect your heart. Although we don't know precisely why laughing helps protect the heart, we do know that mental stress can lead to inflammation, fat build-up in arteries, and, ultimately, heart attacks (Miller, 2000). In this study, researchers compared the humor responses of 300 people. Half of the participants had either had a heart attack or had undergone coronary artery bypass surgery, and the other half were healthy participants without heart disease. Participants answered two questionnaires: one to assess how much or how little they laughed in certain situations and one to measure anger and hostility. The results showed that people with heart disease were less likely to recognize humor or use it to escape uncomfortable situations.

They generally laughed less, even in positive situations, and displayed more anger and hostility (Miller, 2000). This could well explain why fun-loving Santa Claus, AKA 4th-century Greek Christian bishop Saint Nicholas, is still alive and able to work.

Say yes to more laughs and less woes! Routine guffaws work wonders beyond our hearts. Laughing on a regular basis can also significantly affect long-term health conditions.

- **Diabetes**? Laughter therapy delays complications related to cardiovascular disease.
- **Lung problems?** Laughing increases lung capacity by promoting deep breaths, which can help with lung problems and chronic obstructive pulmonary disease (COPD). Boom!
- **Inflammation?** Laughter's got us! It dials down inflammation (as measured by pro-inflammatory cytokine levels) in people with rheumatoid arthritis.
- **Allergen-triggered skin swelling?** Laughter and humor reduce wheal (skin swelling).
- **Mind agility?** In a study that included thirty older adults, humor therapy, AKA a good laugh (watching a twenty-minute humorous movie), improved cognitive function, including learning ability, delayed recall, and visual recognition.
- **Parkinson's disease?** Comedy improv training led to subjective improvements in symptoms for people with Parkinson's disease. WHAT?!

Simple joy, significant impact. It's incredible that something so simple and costs nothing can be so instrumental in helping people. In some hospitals, you may find a professional clown to provide humor and help alleviate anxiety and stress. In 1998, the film *Patch Adams* was filmed on location right down the road from where I lived in Chapel Hill, NC, while in graduate school. My friend Cheryl was an extra in this movie and told me its premise before it was released in theaters. Based on a true story and starring Robin Williams in the titular role, Patch Adams was a doctor and a clown (what an oxymoron). In this feel-good, wacky comedy, Williams' character entertains patients with humor, even though it risks his career. It's a beautiful concept, provided a doctor doesn't deliver any bad news with a big red nose on his face.

I know many people HATE clowns, but imagine if you were walking down the street and a little car pulled up with twenty clowns, each coming out one by one, followed by a goose-honk sound. You'd probably laugh or run screaming. And if more bystanders were around witnessing this, chances are more people would join in and laugh, too, because laughing is contagious. TV producers in the 1950s knew this, and they started adding laugh tracks to sitcoms because they figured if viewers knew when to laugh through prompts, they would find the show more entertaining.

Comedy has long been a staple in television programming, with shows using various techniques to elicit laughter from their audiences. However, recent years have seen a growing interest in the health benefits of laughter beyond entertainment value, leading to the emergence of practices like laughter yoga. Laughter yoga, or Hasya Yoga, involves intentional laughter and breathing exercises to promote physical, emotional, and social well-being. It typically starts with participants' fake laughing, which then turns into real laughing, as you would when a jealous friend makes a disparaging remark about the size of your ass or a boss asks you last minute to work overtime on a Friday. Laughter yoga is easy, requires little instruction, and is quite effective. If it didn't work, you could make it funnier by having everyone dressed as clowns, minions, or Smurfs. But maybe there is no laughter yoga or even yoga where you live. So, how can you incorporate comedy into your life?

After a recent break-up from a very turbulent relationship, my long-time friend Ashlyn felt like a shell of herself. She was always a bit of a worrier, but after her girlfriend dumped her, she couldn't help but overanalyze and obsess over the small details, like when she forgot her birthday. Ashlyn was desperate to find some semblance of comfort and joy, even rewatching her favorite rom-coms, hoping to inspire a moment of happiness (but ended up sobbing hysterically while eating pizza and drinking white wine with ice cubes). Ashlyn would refuse to meet friends, fearing them mentioning her break-up, often citing some ludicrous excuse like having explosive diarrhea that wouldn't let up. One day, the concerned friend I was, I showed up at her door unannounced. I told her I was going to perform stand-up comedy for the first time and would love her to be a beta spectator, to test-watch my routine for moral support. Ashlyn tried using her infamous shit excuse to make me go away, but I offered her some Pepto because I knew Ashlyn had been using this BS IBS excuse for about a month now.

Ashlyn reluctantly agreed to let me in. As she sat watching me "rehearse the show," she found herself laughing, cackling even every twenty seconds or so. My poor girl hadn't laughed in so long that her stomach was aching and her face hurt. She hesitated before replying honestly, "I'm not sure what's funnier. Your ridiculous gestures or the idea that you will try to perform that absurdity in front of a live audience," followed by, "You can't be serious? When did you decide to do stand-up?"

Trying not to overthink her critique, I admitted, "I am not doing stand-up. I will absolutely never be performing that "act." I confessed: "I made it all up. Spontaneous, complete, and utter bullshit. A ruse to get you to let me in!" Ashlyn exploded in hysterics once more (bonus laughter!), and not only did I feel incredible at her laughing her ass off at my absurd antics, but, she felt so much better. She could not believe that I would go to such lengths to try to cheer her up, and in the end, she thanked me and told me that maybe I did have a future in comedy yet.

Needless to say, that was not the last time Ashlyn got treated to a comedy show. Since then, she has seen seasoned pros like Marc Maron, Wanda Sykes, Chris Rock, and Millennial fave, Ali Wong. I also introduced her to my former student, friend, and hilarious comedian in his own right, Powell Mansfield. (Pssst. Google him!) I had helped Ashlyn realize that she could shift the perspective of her girlfriend breaking up with her and enjoy being a single girl again through humor. Comedy has helped both Ashlyn and I reduce the intensity of our negative thoughts and drastically improve our moods.

Laughter yoga and attending stand-up comedy are just some of the novel ways to incorporate comedy into your life. Still, these activities are not for everyone, as we all have a unique sense of humor heavily cultivated by our culture, upbringing, and personality (though who doesn't love a good fart joke?). Humor is commonly known for being subjective; however, if you made it this far, you may have overlooked the use of scatological humor (poop), sex jokes (over-acted orgasms), dancing (twerking, pole, line, moonwalk), and of course our old friends burping and farting.

Stand-up comedians build confidence by dominating the stage and engaging with the audience. Still, I want to emphasize the mental resilience developed from performing over time, which I fiercely admire. Comedians can face rejection, criticism, setbacks, and drunk hecklers, yet they bounce back and keep going. Back in 2018, controversial Australian comedian Jim Jeffries got punched in the face on stage by an angry audience member. The comic briefly left the stage before returning moments later to make jokes about the incident, which generated widespread media attention and arguably propelled his career. The ability to make people laugh is a source of strength, even more so if you can make yourself laugh. Chris Rock was able to do the same thing with the now infamous "Will Smith Oscars Slap" of 2022 and integrated that shocking moment into his 2023 Netflix special.

So, with everything you have learned so far, let's put your new knowledge to the test. Try to write a joke about whatever is at the forefront of your mind, whatever is paining you the most. Pick the second bothersome thing or the third if it's too much. There are many types of jokes, such as observational, one-liners, anecdotal, and deadpan, but the one that works best for the overthinkers is self-deprecating. When you think about writing a joke, it's a lot like telling a story. There are characters, conflict, a beginning, a middle and end, and a resolution. Typically, in comedy, you have two main elements: the set-up (where you detail characters, places, and a situation that sets up the scene) and the punchline (a plot twist where the resolution is something the audience was not expecting). Here are a few helpful tips when it comes to writing a joke:

- **Pick an experience that you too often dwell on.** As an overthinker, you have a million in your thought catalog. Pick one and work from there.
- **Build a premise**. If the experience was something like a time you got stupid drunk, where was it? What happened? Who was there? Many others can relate to being stupid drunk, so you have a winning formula already.

- **Subvert expectations.** This is where you think about the plot twist and exaggerate the shit out of the scenario. So, let's assume you drank too much, and the result was you spent the next two days terrified to check your socials because of drunk messaging to an ex. Lots of folks have been there. But what if your plot twist was you didn't message "how much I miss that divine ass" to *them* but rather to your workplace's GroupMe chat by mistake? The punchline should be short and have an element of surprise. Lead listeners into a false sense of security, and then BAM!
- **Keep it concise**. Deliver on the essentials, but don't spend five minutes discussing the dreaded experience. Take out anything unnecessary.
- **Test it out.** Don't tell people what they think of your joke before telling them, as they will then be ready to critique the shit out of it. The aim is to make them laugh, and if it's under the illusion of a cautionary tale, they hopefully won't see it coming. It's also worth reading the joke aloud, even when nobody is around, so you can gauge what works.

Turning an experience into a self-deprecating joke can offer a new perspective entirely. Writing a joke is optional, but, like many times you have probably pondered before, what's the worst that can happen? With a bit of humor, nothing nearly as wrong as we presume. There have been many times when I look back on the things that filled me with anguish, but now, as a recovering self-saboteur and doomsday scenarist, I laugh. I learned to see the funny side, as cliché as it sounds. So, let's use humor as our weapon to prepare us for the most significant battle and formidable adversary to face: ourselves.

With time and practice, humor will catapult negative thoughts out of your head, like something from medieval times or like a cork popping from a champagne bottle. Then again, when you are in the habit of hopelessness, making jokes may only help temporarily. It's best to grab over-thinking by its evil devil horns and confront it once and for all. In the next chapter, we delve deep into how to recognize overthinking, challenge the train of negative thoughts, and finally put the fucking brakes on it (and ideally, not the emergency brake).

––––––

Key takeaway: Humor has healing power. There is science behind how laughing can improve mental resilience and help you overcome overthinking. Lean on that and learn to harness it.

CHAPTER TWO

TAMING THE OVERTHINKING BEAST: DISCOVERING IT'S NOT AS SCARY AS IT SEEMS

ME: "WHAT COULD POSSIBLY GO WRONG?"
My anxiety: "I'm glad you asked." — Unknown

Remember the joys of youth when it was so simple just to let certain shit go? I mean, if the viral Disney song "Let It Go" from *Frozen* can celebrate the magic of moving on, we should also be able to. You were mooching off your parents, so you didn't have to worry as much about money; leaving a minimum-wage job crushing your soul was a lot easier when you were 18; you probably weren't the one buying groceries and making dinner when you were ten either. Nope. You didn't concern yourself with that stuff. You probably didn't overthink nearly as much. But our minds can get cluttered once exposed to the harsh realities of adulting and all the burdens that come with it. And that stress wears on us. What? You mean I have to pay for my $7 coffee at Starbucks myself? What? Food won't magically appear in my fridge once I am on my own, and my dinner won't cook itself? There is nothing like going to a laundromat and learning about the lost sock vortex the hard way to make you appreciate the "ignorance is bliss" wonderland of many people's younger days. Indeed, by now, as adults, we probably all have some mental resilience to work with to manage overthinking better, so let's dive in.

First, let's look at what exactly overthinking is, which you've probably already thought about numerous times. I thought I knew what overthinking was, but I was over-thinking *overthinking* so much that the overthinking about *overthinking* was overthinking. Sorry, I couldn't resist. You've probably had someone tell you you are overthinking, and maybe you politely told them to suck it. But what the heck is it?

Overthinking refers to repetitive, unproductive thought, particularly ruminating about the past and present and worrying about the future. In other words, it is a consistent loop of thoughts that never seem to stop or have a resolution. It's annoying, frustrating, and bothersome; it can disrupt your entire plans for the day. It's a massive pain in the ass. You lose sleep, you lose willpower, and you lose yourself. Over-thinking can dictate every aspect of our lives, from the past to the present to the future. To gain some clarity here, let us better understand why:

- **The past:** Here, we have our regrets and resentments. At these moments, we wish we had made a different choice in life or can't shake off a feeling of embarrassment from a million years ago. The term "rumination" is often used by researchers to describe the experience of unproductive thoughts based on the past. Whether it was yesterday or a year ago, dwelling on the past will not help shape your life in the present or future.
- **The present:** Here, we contemplate something related to the present, such as our personality,

identity, circumstances, or relationships. You might ponder if you were in the right kind of relationship or over-focus on what you perceive as your flaws. You might have thought about how your co-worker was rude ten minutes ago and fantasized about how you could have responded (such as taking off your shoe and throwing it at them).

- **The future:** Here, we stress about something short-term, like an upcoming presentation or a doctor's appointment about hemorrhoids. Maybe it's something long-term, such as how some of us questioned our existence or purpose during the COVID-19 lockdown, or it could be anxiety about the inability to find true love from watching too many Netflix dramas. Regardless, our worries are not helping us; they stagnate our progress.

I know it all sounds like a tarot reading from a fortune teller, but we all overthink something. It's just that some of us do it more than others. Like, a lot more. If you have ADHD like me, then you're likely an overthinking expert. We might be fixated on the past, present, future, or all of them simultaneously. And when your brain is causing a drain, it can seem like there is no way out. Maybe the thing that always bothered me the most was how overthinking could creep up out of the blue without any warning. I can recall a time when I was sitting in a restaurant for lunch. I was alone, and there weren't many people inside (I made sure of this by looking through the window before going in). The server floated over and handed me the menu, and I ordered a soup and sandwich on sourdough bread (For once, I did not overthink my decision of what to order!). As I glanced from table to table, I spotted an older man looking directly at me, helping manifest my overthinking faster than boiling water. Then came the *what ifs*; what if there is some shit on my face? What if he sits beside me and asks me to join some cult? What if he was the dude I flipped the bird to when he tried jaywalking as I drove? There were so many ideas rushing through my head. I opened the menu to cover my face while ogling the wine selection. I probably thought: "An entire bottle of Pinot Noir feels like a fantastic choice right about now."

As I slowly tilted the menu, the man was *still* fixated on me. I raised an eyebrow at him and even mustered up the courage to give out a tut. Wait a sec. He was pointing and counting now! Was he rating me out of 10? I stood up, ready to rush out faster than The Flash on his way to a crime scene. As I turned around, I noticed a blackboard with the menu specials. He wasn't looking at me; he was looking at what was behind me: the freaking chalkboard menu! I sat back down again, pretending that I was rearranging the seat. Even though he wasn't looking at me, I couldn't stop thinking about raising my eyebrow for hours and tutting hours after.

Overthinking, just like many other things in life, *seems* harder to quit as we barrel out of control toward midlife and beyond, but there are a myriad of reasons why we struggle to quit anything, such as:

- **Habits become more ingrained:** We tend to develop more ingrained habits in our daily routines over time. These habits can be difficult to break or recognize, as they have become automatic and require less conscious effort. This results in us finding it more challenging to quit things that have become habitual, such as smoking, drinking, overeating, or overthinking.
- **Fear of change:** As we get older, we sometimes become set in our ways and less open to change or taking risks. This can make it harder to quit things,

as we may fear the unknown or feel uncertain about the future. It doesn't help when you have financial commitments such as a mortgage or children.

- **Increased stress:** As we age, we may experience more stress, making quitting harder. We don't want stress as we age, as we know it potentially leads to anxiety and depression, which makes breaking habits or making significant lifestyle changes challenging.

Yep, you would think as we ripen that we can handle anything life throws at us, that we can get back up after falling like Rocky in Rocky, Rocky 2, Rocky 3, Rocky 4, and Rocky 5. But we can get so knocked out from feeling overwhelmed that we revert to finding comfort in the most straightforward ways possible. It's why we procrastinate by playing 2048, Tetris, and Solitaire online, eating frozen pizzas for dinner, and binge-watching trashy shit on Netflix.

While we can hyper-focus on the most minute details, having such an overactive imagination can also be a great thing. You wouldn't marry someone you met today tomorrow unless they were super rich and like 98 years old, or you were in Las Vegas and lost a bet. I can recall so many moments when someone told me I was "thinking too much" or "you are just overthinking," but then found out I was right all along. Surely, if there is too much thinking, there can also be too little? I like to think there are times when it is good; some may call it intuition, and others may call it rationality. I call it clarity.

A great example is if you ever planned on traveling for an extended period. If you tried to wing it, you'd probably have wasted your budget within the first week. So you seek clarity by thinking, but instead of getting overwhelmed by negative thoughts, you take action, set a few goals, or talk it out with someone. You don't conjure up ridiculous scenarios like getting chased by mobsters or getting an awkward pat down at the airport for carrying gum; you think about what you need to do and thus better prepare yourself for the trip.

Hold up for a second, though! What if you keep on thinking, though? What if negative thought after negative thought consumes you? For too many years, I never really celebrated my birthday. I mean, as we get a bit older, it's not nearly as extravagant as getting your parents' old car when we turn 16 or when you turn 21 in the US and having your first legal tequila shot, followed by the second and the third, then the … oh shit, where was I? But when my birthday was around the corner, I often became withdrawn. I hated the idea of friends forgetting my birthday or just lumping it in with Christmas as it had more or less constantly been as a child, or simply the fact that people go out of town for the holidays and no one is around to celebrate anyway (the plight of having a birthday within days of Christmas). I would assume nobody cared about me or didn't know me well enough to really "get" me. I had convinced myself in my overthinking that celebrating my birthday was a waste of time.

And yet, deep down, I wanted to be surrounded by friends and family. But if I *did* have a party, and nobody came, could I overcome that? Because that did happen to me once, and it was brutal. But this time a few years ago, I didn't even need to contemplate such an idea because, on my big day, I woke up to cards, cake, and gifts from my kids and partner, texts from my siblings, friends, and colleagues, and a card in the mail from my dad with some cold hard cash inside. Everyone surrounded me, sang to me, and told me how much they appreciated me. Later, my kids took me out for coffee and lunch, and I didn't pay for a single thing. My overthinking made me miss out on so much, and I am sure it has for many others, too. This was one of many times that taught me to live in the moment and make a conscious effort to thwart overthinking.

The same shit has happened to me time and time again. Once, I was supposed to attend a friend's baby shower, like before I had my kids. And let me tell you, before I had kids, I was not a baby person, not in the slightest. I had never even been to one before and ruminated on gift ideas, hoping to get something worthy of such a "prestigious' ' event but also something cool and edgier. But, I had to settle for a run-of-the-mill classic teddy bear since it was last minute. I mean, I didn't want to go there empty-handed. I could still show up for support. Instead of persevering for the few hours it lasted, I told my friend that I was ill. My friend was disheartened, but what could she do? I needed to rest. It was self-sabotage at its worst, and I dwelled on this decision for years after.

The problem is that we can't deal with our overthinking unless we fully know why it's happening. To fully understand why we overthink, we need to take a proactive approach to recognizing and knowing the brooding reasons before our overactive brain explodes. In my case, I got an ADHD diagnosis very late in life, and suddenly, my whole life and all my overthinking made sense. But regardless of your diagnosis or lack thereof, let's discuss it. If you experience any of the following, it's getting too much:

- **Difficulty focusing on a particular task**. You might be trying to work on a spreadsheet, but the data you enter is in your head and not on the computer. You could even try watering a houseplant but pause momentarily to remember how you spilled wine all over the former French Minister of Equal Opportunity at a dinner you hosted for him when you were a professor and also almost made him miss his flight the next day because you drove him to the wrong airport … I shit you not. Those things *really* happened. But even if you are simply dwelling on thoughts like "Did I give my neighbor's cat enough food?" or "Is my ex going to message me after drunk messaging them saying they are a massive narcissistic jerk," the struggle is real, even more so when your head starts doing mental vomiting. The problem with this type of thinking is that it pops up out of the blue, throwing you off anything you've been working on. Worse still, when it is constantly happening, it encourages you to procrastinate, and the tasks you planned to work on go to shit, or if you do try to work on them, the quality of work goes to shit.

- **Difficulty falling asleep.** This is a big one for many, and it involves all of the "what if" moments we have grown to cherish. So many times, I could not sleep because my mind wouldn't shut the hell up. Sometimes, I would relive a painful memory; other times, I struggled to get some shut-eye as I was terrified about the future. And the more I added to the list in my head, the harder it was to sleep; it's like counting sheep, except the sheep represent stress. Lack of sleep profoundly affects your well-being, and if you don't get enough sleep, you end up feeling like an extra from *The Walking Dead*.

- **Difficulty relaxing.** You want to sit outside on a sunny day and read that book you've been putting off for three years, but as you set aside your phone, it beeps. You want to turn off the phone but then worry about emergencies, so put it on silent instead. As you read, you are worried about getting disrupted by a call or text, even if the phone is on silent. Overthinking can make it so hard to relax; even if you decide to free up some time to do something enjoyable, you can catch yourself having a mental battle worse than Dwight Schrute trying to decipher sarcasm or, better yet, Gareth Keenan trying to convince his co-workers that he can kill a man with a single blow. (All apologies if you have never watched the American version of *The Office* or, my preference, the original British *Office*. Google that shit.)

- **Heavily impacted or impaired mood.** Perpetual overthinking can cause guilt, anger, and envy. Some people become sensitive because they focus on negative thoughts in an endless loop. They might even hold a grudge due to overanalyzing things people say or do.
- **Dwelling on mistakes.** We all make mistakes; we are only human, after all. But as an overthinker, a simple mistake is amplified, deconstructed, and, more commonly, misinterpreted. Through this mistake or a multitude of them, you can feel guilty or remorseful, assuming that beating yourself up is the best way to stop yourself from repeating the error.
- **Overanalyzing anything you say or have said.** Even when mentally mulling, we can hyper-focus on the words we use, leading to delayed responses, an inability to make choices, or fear of making mistakes. You may also use your free time trying to decipher a "hidden meaning" behind something someone has said.
- **Focusing on the shit that's out of your control.** We may have no control over what others do or say

(unless you are a hypnotist), but we can focus on what we can control. That is much better than getting anxious and stressed about all the shit you have no power over.

Phew! It's like going down memory lane before coming to that end scene in *Thelma and Louise*, from which you should hit reverse and never look back (or is it forward?). Whether you are going forward, backward, up, down, sideways, or reverse cowgirl, you can quit overthinking and quit it for good. The best thing is that it doesn't involve a frontal lobotomy. Negative thoughts can not only affect us emotionally and mentally; they can dictate our lives and how we choose to live. It's imperative to understand that while negativity clouds our minds sometimes, it is possible to overcome it without becoming one of those toxic positivity assholes. I want to emphasize the benefits of quitting; think of this as a punk rock morale-boosting realistic "pep" talk. Pep isn't a very punk word, but never mind that. Here are some things you can look forward to:

- **Better sleep, and much more of it.** Imagine going to bed any freaking time you wanted. That is one of the most overlooked perks of adulting, really … that, and eating an entire cake in one sitting. By ending overthinking, you can finally free yourself from the mental traffic jams (and all the asshole drivers that are your thoughts honking their horns) that hinder a restful night's sleep. No more wild, chaotic thoughts racing through your head or waking up in the middle of the night shouting, "It was drunk me, not real me!"
- **Better relationships.** Maybe when a friend tells us we are being silly, they don't mean we are a

complete idiot. We stop misinterpreting assumptions and try communicating like a healthier, happier person. By not overthinking, we can truly listen and understand what others are saying without our thoughts getting in the way. This leads to stronger and healthier relationships with friends, family, and significant others.

- **Better decisions.** No more hesitations or lame-ass excuses that make you feel guilt and shame. We make choices with conviction and confidence. We learn to trust our instincts instead of randomly picking one of 100 scenarios. Flip imposter syndrome the bird. They deserve it.

- **Increased productivity, AKA getting shit done.** How often have you spent hours worrying about a task instead of actually doing it? For some, this is just class par for the course ADHD analysis paralysis. Whether it's ADHD-induced or isolated neurotypical circumstance-driven anxiety, it can happen to anyone. When your head is stuck in negative thoughts, you are distracted. Dwelling is spending too much time on shit you can't do much about and not focusing on taking action toward things you can. By letting go of overthinking, we can focus on the task at hand and complete it more efficiently. No more second-guessing every decision or getting stuck in analysis paralysis. We can trust ourselves to make decisions and take action without the constant fear of failure or scrutiny.

- **Fewer worries.** Okay, there are still some, but fewer for sure. And irrationality has gone out the window. You experience less stress and anxiety because you experience fewer negative thoughts.

And if you need therapy and/or medication to get there, that's okay! I do both. But I also laugh a lot. Laughter is one of the most essential therapeutic anxiety hacks in my toolbox. And for once, I'm not joking!

By this point, we understand why it's hard to quit over-thinking, how to recognize when shit is getting too much, and the benefits of kicking overthinking to the curb, leaving us with mental freedom. In the next chapter, we bypass all the negative thoughts and empower ourselves enough to navigate the life we want and really need.

———

Key takeaway: Quitting overthinking has benefits. Overthinking in moderation can be a good thing, but learn to recognize when overthinking has become too much.

CHAPTER THREE

THE ART OF MENTAL DECLUTTERING: KICK ANXIETY TO THE CURB AND EMBRACE THE UNPREDICTABLE

"TRYING to make sense of my own musings is like trying to read anything these days without my damn glasses – utterly pointless!" — Sara Toninstan (yeah, I'm quoting myself! Deal with it, b*tches!)

It might seem not that long ago that we were forced to embrace uncertainty, no thanks to a shitty virus. I mean, what I am now calling "The Great Covid Lockdown of 2020" was a trying time for us all. Don't get me wrong: working from home was fun initially, and you could walk around in your pajamas all day. Then that fun fizzled out, especially when you realized neighbors who were once friends were in a civil war over toilet paper. I even considered staring sternly from my window and giving the neighbor's kids the middle finger, hoping they would TP my house in retaliation. I figured that was too risky; if they didn't have toilet paper to throw, they might just use shit. Kids are good at finding shit, too; they pretend they are going to play detective armed with magnifying glasses, but in reality, they are galavanting like horses through the park, searching for fresh turds. When lockdown finally ended, it felt surreal, as though I was the orca from Free Willy jumping over the barrier and into the ocean, or for me, into a bar.

Throughout history, human civilization has faced uncertainty. The global financial crisis of 2008 caused a brutal recession. The world went to war twice, too. And on top of that was the Great Depression, which is self-explanatory. Even now, we have never-ending sequels to *The Fast and The Furious*, and you want to scream, "JUST LET IT DIE!" The bottom line is that no matter the hand dealt, history has shown that we can face uncertainty and persevere. So, is it possible to embrace uncertainty when, as an overthinker, you want to predict and control every outcome?

In today's world, new dilemmas and scenarios bombard us daily, such as wondering whether AI will replace your job or openly admitting that growing avocados isn't good for the environment and facing backlash. Thankfully, we have come a long way from the hardships faced by our ancestors, and the magic of science has uncovered something about our brain that finally explains why we have a stronger relationship with negative thoughts than positive ones.

It all comes down to evolution. In our prehistoric days, as primitive hairy beings, it was imperative to register threats to survive. Anyone who could avoid danger and thus death stayed alive long enough to pass this instinctive trait genetically, which is still with us today. Negativity bias, or the negativity effect, is our brain's tendency to be impacted more by adverse events than positive ones, with some studies showing that there is more electrical activity in our brain when focused on negative stimuli than positive ones. Overthinking and negativity bias share some similarities.

However, while overthinking is the tendency to dwell so much on thoughts or worries that you end up overwhelmed and unable to take action, negativity bias causes you to overlook a positive experience or downplay it over a negative one, leading to negative thoughts and behaviors. An overthinker will over-analyze or misinterpret the positive experience, discount it, and consequently struggle to stop thinking about it. Someone can overthink without having a negative bias and vice versa. Then again, having a negative bias can sometimes lead to overthinking. So, to summarize:

- Overthinking involves replaying events in your head, analyzing every possible outcome, and stressing out about the future.
- Negativity bias involves negatively interpreting events and focusing on those negative aspects of the event, which can, but not always, contribute to overthinking.

I remember my first party after the lockdown. I can't say I would usually attend social gatherings much. Still, after being cooped up like a sad hen for so long, I convinced myself otherwise. I knew only a handful of people, and though I yearned to reside in a corner and wait it out, the corners were occupied already (with probable overthinkers who arrived earlier than me). This guy who noticed I was alone approached me, and I introduced myself. After a minute, the guy pardoned himself and walked away. As I stared at his back, I instantly wondered if this was a sign that maybe I had done something or said something wrong. As I gazed around the room, I spotted a few other party attendees glancing over, further making me paranoid. "I must have done something wrong!" I thought. But what could it have been? Had my chronic RBF surfaced too obviously again? Maybe I should smile like a freakin' jack-o-lantern on their honeymoon for the next person who approached me. Maybe smiling too much might make people think I am on drugs. It was getting to be too much. I pulled out my phone and pretended to take an emergency call, pointing my phone to people and waving simultaneously like a terrible phone salesperson. My negativity bias made me misinterpret the situation, which made me contemplate it for hours once I left.

According to psychologist Dr. Rick Hanson, "the mind is like Velcro for negative experiences and Teflon for positive ones" (2013). We observe negative bias in a variety of ways, such as:

- Remembering insults more than praise
- Being highly skeptical of new people, places, or things
- Giving more importance to negative events than positive ones
- Noticing adverse events and recalling them with detail over positive ones

But, enough about negativity already. Negative thoughts interfere with everyday activities, make us lose sleep, and ultimately prevent us from enjoying life. I couldn't even go to a party. Parties are supposed to be where you go for free food (and drink free booze if that's your thing). The following day, a friend told me that the guy I thought had disappeared because of me had actually left because he spotted his ex. Good news for me, bad news for him.

Letting go of negative thoughts is different for everyone, and what worked for me may not work for you. Strategies and "happiness hacks" that may seem fool-proof for neurotypical brains aren't always well suited to neurodivergent brains, well-intentioned though they are. That said, I can't stress enough (pun intended, in a good way) how pivotal humor is in dealing with negative thoughts despite how your brain is wired. For example, consider some of these awesome strategies (some truly absurdly remarkable):

- **Watch or listen to something funny.** Suppose you are stuck in an overthinking mood or having a shit day. In that case, a few minutes watching a video or listening to a funny podcast can give you a much-needed break from reality. I recommend watching classic Vine videos, as they are iconic and silly. **Action:** Consider following a social media account notorious for funny videos and skits.
- **Tell a joke.** The internet is full of cringe-worthy jokes and puns, and it's worth cherry-picking some favorites. You might even get a job promotion by telling a dad joke. Who knows? **Action:** Write a joke about something that you overthink. This exercise will give you perspective, and you will see it more positively.
- **Exchange memes.** Nothing breaks up a monotonous day at work better than receiving a juicy meme. If you run out of memes, try making one. Heck, I even have a whole folder of my favorite memes. It's like having a family album, though I cringe less when looking over the memes than when looking over my family photo album. **Action:** Make a meme folder and ask friends to send you their best memes.
- **Spend time with funny people.** Whether it's your best friend, sibling, or grumpy grandma with cataracts who thinks you had a nose job, funny people uplift your mood and offer a fresh perspective on the bullshit perplexing you. **Action:** Spend more time with someone who always makes you laugh.

- **Practice laughing.** Make a conscious effort to laugh, such as standing in front of a mirror and making the most ridiculous faces ever. Hell, do impressions of Shrek or Donkey to get the laughs out. Or better yet, do impressions of TV and film characters doing impressions of other characters, like when Jim imitates Dwight in the American version of *The Office* or when Zuko imitates Uncle Iroh and Azula in *Avatar the Last Airbender*. And if you have no idea what I'm talking about, it doesn't matter. Pick your favorite funny characters to imitate. And if you don't watch many TV shows or movies, just imitate your sibling or best friend. It might be more amusing if you imitate them in person, though. **Action:** Don't be afraid; just try it. TRY IT NOW!

- **Tell a one-minute story.** This activity is an excellent way to engage with another person. It often serves as a warm-up technique in improv comedy, and I also used it a lot in teaching with my students. You make up a story in one minute, and then the other person must recall everything you said. **Action:** Before doing this exercise, try to think of the most outrageous concepts with small details, making it hard for a friend to recall everything (but also very funny).

- **Release a 1-minute rant.** Oh man, anyone who knows me knows I love a good rant. Look around you and pick an object or word for inspiration. Once you have decided on something, go on a 1-minute rant while also adopting a solid character. It could be anything from the color of your wall to watching a neighbor's garden. The more mundane, the better. After it's complete, pick something else to rant about. **Action:** Look up wild stories from trashy news websites like TMZ or the Daily Mail for inspiration. Or just follow your national politics for two minutes. I'm sure you'll find something rant-worthy quickly.

- **Unleash your fury in a rage room.** Also known as an anger room, it's an entertainment venue where you can sometimes smash the shit out of plates, furniture, and even cars. It's a pretty cathartic way to let off steam. **Action:** Make one in your backyard if you can't find one. I once threw dishes at a tree outside my house. I missed with most of them, but the intention was there.

- **Try trash journals.** A trash journal is a book where you can write about anything and everything without censorship. That includes swear words. HELL FUCKING YES. If you saw the movie *Mean Girls*, you've probably seen the burn book; well, it was a trash journal of sorts. **Action:** Get yourself a journal and let those creative juices flow.

- **Hang out with a pet.** Animals are hilarious; dogs sniff your butt to shake hands, and cats sit on your face when you try to sleep to kill you. Seriously. My dog has no idea how pivotal a role he plays in my mental well-being, but it is massive. If you don't own a pet, visit a friend who does; they probably love the attention their beloved companion gets anyway. **Action:** If you have no pet, consider going to a cat cafe or dog park. You can also visit your local animal shelter.

- **Paint with your feet.** Painting can help, but trying it with your feet is even more hilarious. You could make something so cool and unique that it could be worth hanging on your mini-fridge. **Action:** Try doing a painting with your feet, a self-portrait. If you're an ADHDer like me, you may already use your toes and feet for picking up shit off the floor, turning off the space heater in front of you, or for stimming, grasping the coffee table for dear life, toe knuckles clenched so hard they're turning red, so why not try painting?

- **Play a prank.** I am not talking about leaving a bag of flaming dog shit on someone's porch. Still, you can do something simple like hide two of your friend's things but tell them that you hid three, or replace your friend's framed family photos with photos of your favorite funny actor or cartoon character. Changing someone's computer screen/screensaver is always an innocently fun one, too, so long as you keep it kind and clean, not mean and dirty. Playing pranks is akin to channeling your inner rebellious teen, and it's nothing short of exhilarating! **Action:** Check YouTube for ideas, but play it safe, and don't be an asshole.

- **Dress up.** We all need healthy distractions from time to time. One great way is to raid your closet and dress up. When you look good, you feel good, right? **Action:** Consider wearing your partner's clothes to see their reaction. Hell, I put my dog's shirt on once, and it was hilarious.

- **Play with AI.** Heaps of AI services are now available for entertainment. Midjourney is awesome for conjuring images about anything you prompt it to, and you can use ChatGPT to ask about all kinds of weird topics. Go wild! The more ridiculous the prompts, the more absurd the resulting scenarios! You can also see where your conversations with Siri (if you have an iPhone) or Alexa (if you have this Amazon VA at your service) go. You'd be surprised at how deadpan and hilarious they can be. **Action:** Sign up for the free version of ChatGPT or Midjourney and let your creativity run wild.

- **Larp yourself into laughter.** Also known as live-action role-play, adults dress up and act out scenes. You can be a Viking, a witch, or even a hobbit if you have big, smelly feet. **Action:** Check online for any larping events close to you.

- **Twerk it out.** You think I'm kidding? Think again. Dancing makes us happy, but if you can't dance, then simply twerk. Have you ever twerked to your favorite song? Why not give it a go and see how you feel after?**Action:** Pick a short song (depending on how fit you are, twerking to the 10-minute version of Taylor Swift's *All Too Well* will literally become a pain in the ass), and shake that booty.

- **Color your stress away.** Indeed, there are coloring books for adults, and some are remarkably well done. If you have yet to hone your drawing, painting, or twerking skills, this may be your golden opportunity to unleash your creativity! **Action:** Check online or at your local bookstore for adult coloring books.

For some, these ideas (a few of which are admittedly a bit outlandish) will work; for others, maybe less. The point is incorporating humor has helped me enormously in dealing with negative thoughts and an ADHD brain, and yet, while comedy can give us a fresh perspective, it can sometimes only provide short-term relief. Good habits and self-awareness can extinguish negative thoughts in the long term. One great habit is practicing self-acceptance. We all need to learn to accept that what we did in the past was when we didn't know what we do today and that we probably did not have access to the right resources. That version of you is not the same person as today. We can try to resist, but then we prolong our recovery and ability to feel better. Practicing acceptance requires surrendering yourself without resistance. If you deal with an asshole at work, instead of worrying about future situations with them, accept that they will never change, regardless of how much you attempt to please that annoying asshole. Acceptance is acknowledging and allowing a problem to be what it is without resistance or trying to change it.

I learned that I have ADHD very late in life, and this knowledge has played a crucial role in my newfound self-acceptance. I now know that I am not broken and that my brain is actually wired differently than a neurotypical brain. I now understand the reasons behind my overthinking. But more importantly, I have learned to accept myself fully both despite and in light of my ADHD diagnosis. By practicing acceptance, we can become more comfortable with uncertainty, which, when we embrace it, is a total game-changer, giving us freedom and opening up a whole new world of possibilities.

Have you ever visited an amusement park, state fair, or carnival with loads of rides, games, and cotton candy? They can be really fun, right? Well, not when you are an overthinker anticipating things like mechanical failures or getting food poisoning, or you experience sensory overload and find the crowds of people horrifying, but other than that, yeah, fun.

Here's a personal amusement park story: I was meeting my friend Danny for a night of madness and mayhem eons ago. Danny was terrified of going on anything that involved his legs over his head. For once, I was not the overthinker. One thing about lots of us ADHDers is we love to chase dopamine, take risks, and be spontaneous. As a teenager, I worked at an amusement park and loved the craziest, fastest coasters out there. As an adult, that remains more or less unchanged, though I don't live close to an amusement park anymore. Anyway, I was super enthusiastic about experiencing the biggest and "scariest" rides with Danny. I knew he didn't want to be a party pooper, but I could also tell that he worried the jig would be up sooner or later.

He couldn't believe he was entertaining the idea of going on a ride. Still, after watching people NOT blast off their seats like a rocket, he assumed it might be semi-safe after all. We got into some kind of whirly-girly thing. It looked like a spider, but at least to Danny, it didn't go too high. We got into our seats, and he panicked mentally (when you yourself are a professional panicker, you know the signs!) when the ride attendant checked to ensure the lap bar was locked. I think he thought he couldn't breathe for a moment, and before he could say anything, we started spinning. I exploded joyously, but Danny's screaming manifested in terrified tears running down his face. I was seriously concerned for him, at least for the first few seconds, but I calmed down when I saw that he realized he would not fall out of his seat, haha! As we spun around and around, up, down, left, right, and counter-clockwise, though, one of my shoes flew off my foot and into the air, and poof! It was gone.

Once my shoe vanished into thin air, * I * stopped enjoying the ride and started worrying about where it went. Dammit, I wanted my shoe back. I couldn't walk around with only one shoe, and worse, what would everyone there think of me? As the ride decelerated, we came to a halt. I told Danny about my shoe flying off, and he just laughed. I still wouldn't stop stressing until I got my beloved shoe back. We searched all over but to no avail. My shoe was gone, and though Danny told me to stop worrying and that he was ready to go on other rides, I insisted that we needed to go and went home instead. (WTF?! Really, Sara? Yeah. Really.)

I never expected my shoe to fly off into oblivion, nor did I expect my friend to think I should carry on without one. But looking back, I realize that even though I was only wearing one shoe, I still could have had a good time. I am sure I am not the only person who has lost a shoe during a carnival ride. For all I know, there could have been a flip-flop shop or some stand selling hideous Crocs in these situations. And I could have gone to the lost and found and rifled through all the unclaimed stuff and possibly found a shoe that not only came in my size but was also the same heel height and for the right foot. Ok, maybe not, but you get where I'm going here. If I had just accepted the situation and not felt embarrassed, perhaps I could have had so much more fun because Danny had miraculously mustered the courage to go on the bigger rides only to have me deflate his courage and my initial excitement over a fucking shoe. Note to self and pro tip: always keep a complete change of clothes and an extra pair of shoes in your car. You just never know. But I digress. If only I had embraced uncertainty instead of fighting against it, sigh.

You'd think that the pandemic would have trained us to expect the unexpected when, in reality, it made us worse off. Would you cancel everything if you planned a whole day but discovered it *might* rain? I say embrace it with an umbrella. Humans crave knowledge about the future; maybe knowing how to live with insecurity is the only security. Let's embrace uncertainty like you lost your shoe at the fair, but instead of rushing home, you own it. It could even become a fashion trend if you flaunt it enough. Wouldn't you wonder how your day would have worked out with one shoe? Wouldn't it make such a great story? It'd be better than this one, where I just gave up and went home. I realize that maybe walking around an amusement park with one shoe isn't *that* realistic. But I ultimately gave up. I could have gone home, changed, and come back. Right? My point is ultimately this: don't we grow more out of our comfort zone and thus build resilience when we learn to reframe adversity?

Here are a few truisms and some advice for when life decides to pour down rain on you:

- **You are not a Swiss army knife.** A Swiss army knife can fix almost anything, but not in life. When shit hits the fan, we want someone to rescue us. Okay, that would be more rational if you were in a burning building or got lost in IKEA. When facing uncertainty, though, we need to stop complaining and divert our attention from fixating on the problem to focusing on the outcome we need. If not, we will stay stuck and unable to move forward. For example, your cat could run away. You could focus on finding the fleeing fur ball or choose to do nothing, hoping they have not been catnapped and may return one day.
- **Why say WHY when you can say WHY NOT?** We can conjure every worst-case scenario during uncertain times, leading to more stress. We grieve for things not lost or panic when things have not reached boiling point. But how about instead thinking about the opposite? What if things DO turn out just fine? Do you ever stress out about meeting an old friend you haven't seen in years, wondering if they've changed? What if they immediately tell you how much they've missed you and are excited about your life's updates instead?

- **Prepare, don't pontificate**. It's hard when we don't know what to expect around the corner. In fact, we might avoid corners altogether. What can help is having a plan. We ADHDers crave and need a solid routine, even if we resist it. It can help us feel in control and adapt to uncertainty. Suppose you were to meet an ex-partner and debate who gets to keep a signed Nickelback record, with a plan instead of expectations. In that case, you could at least know what to do if you both don't meet eye to eye. Expectations set us up for failure. If you expect to get the record because you have a Chad Kroeger/Nickelback tramp stamp, then you probably won't, but it might just work if you plan to get it if you give a signed Smash mouth record in return. (No offense to big fans, but I needed a reference point here!)

- **Face it with fire.** We should reassure ourselves that we can face anything life throws at us. Whatever big problem might show up, you've probably handled worse ones. If the worst is yet to come, you've come a long way not to back down now, right? Have you ever noticed in superhero movies how the hero always seems to pull off the impossible after remembering some impactful phrase? It's cliché, sure, but it's a testament to the power of words. Do that, but for yourself.

- **Resistance is futile.** I know there is a Star Trek joke I could throw in here somewhere, but we need to stay focused! We live at a time when uncertainty has ironically never been more certain. We've got global warming, AI replacing jobs, and human imaginations, for that matter, and obsolete face masks you can't use for toilet paper. The world is changing rapidly, and growth requires adaptability. Refusing change amplifies emotions and halts progress. We must be open to learning and evolving as individuals to thrive in a dynamic environment. The alternative? Acceptance. Acceptance gives us a reality check, seeing what is in the present moment and giving us the power to move forward. To become more accepting, we must surrender and accept the situation. It doesn't mean things will get worse or better. Still, at that moment, you likely have no control over the problem, so it's not worth worrying further about it.

Uncertainty is a natural part of life and provides us with opportunities for growth and learning. By accepting the unknown, we can focus on setting realistic goals that are attainable and flexible enough to adjust to changing circumstances. Goals give us direction and a sense of purpose, too. If we want to adapt to uncertainty and life, it's worth figuring out how we can use goal setting to seek challenges as opportunities to empower us further. It all sounds a bit deep, and in a way, it is, but I shall reveal it all in the next chapter. Or will I? That's just a little taster to see if you can embrace uncertainty.

———

Key takeaway: Let go of your negative thoughts and embrace uncertainty.

CHAPTER FOUR

GET YOUR SH*T TOGETHER
ON YOUR OWN TERMS

"OVERTHINKING IS like playing a driving video game; you sit behind the wheel and steer, but you *literally* go nowhere. So set some realistic goals, and maybe save those quarters for Ms. Pac-Man. Or an actual car." — Sara Toninstan (yeah, I quoted myself again)

The year was 2020, and I mean officially 2020. The clock turned midnight, and everybody screamed and shouted, "Happy New Year." After all the hugging and shrugging, I had a moment to reflect. Happy New Year indeed, except I couldn't stop thinking about all these big plans I made. I had spent several days desperately crafting a list of things I hoped to achieve. Most people did, right? But here's the thing: New Year's Resolutions are a joke for many people, a lie we whisper to ourselves. Because deep down inside, we don't actually believe we can accomplish them. We have yet to convince ourselves of what needs to be done and that we will make it happen. Writing down what you want to achieve at the beginning of the year or any time in life is much more worthwhile and realistic if you also write down what you're willing to sacrifice and what you intend to change.

The first thing to understand is that your present self is an accumulation of your past habits and daily actions. So, if you want to change, you actually have to *change*. This pertains to every aspect of your life. But know this: change does not happen overnight, and you don't have to change everything all at once. Many of the goals I included on my list for 2020 were pretty universally standard:

- Get back into pre-pandemic shape (yeah, I, like so many, embraced a more sedentary life in 2020)
- Drink less
- Read more books that aren't for work in any way
- Spend less time on social media (I was already a lurker/voyeur anyway)
- Spend more time with friends
- Write a book about my overthinking brain

Sound familiar? Out of the things on that list, I only achieved one, and not even in 2020. Or 2021 or 2022. Can you guess which one?! 2020 was fraught with the global Coronavirus pandemic and was, ironically, the Chinese Year of the Pig. It's almost like fate, really. We are all guilty of setting resolutions we never reach, especially days before a new year, with the big problem of sticking to them. You may have downloaded a few books you thought you would get around to reading but have yet to do so. Maybe you upgraded to Super Duolingo because you wanted to learn five new languages, but you never got past the Spanish you already knew from high school. You may have tried going to a packed gym on January 2nd but couldn't find parking, so you went home.

We set self-expectations but commonly set the bar so high

that we can barely reach it. If you are a neurodivergent over-thinker like me, you are used to disappointment from setting expectations that you feel like you never meet. Insert fist bumps here for solidarity with all my overthinking late-diag-nosed ADHDers.

We tend to be all-or-nothing perfectionists, which makes us more anxious and causes us to ruminate on the what-ifs. But just because we *can* analyze something doesn't mean we should. While self-expectations refer to the standards we set based on beliefs, values, and desires, realistic expectations are based on your abilities and circumstances. Much of the advice out there, books and blogs about crushing your goals and implementing habit-changing productivity hacks, etc., often don't work for neurodiverse overthinking pros because it frequently originates from neurotypical perspectives, whether they're from doctors, therapists, life coaches, or comedians, who all have good intentions, an ADHDer's brain chemistry is actually different. Yes, our brains are wired differently. How we think and process information is different, and these differences stem from the unique structure and chemistry of the ADHD brain. Scientists now also believe that we are born this way. I failed at my New Year's resolutions like many others because, like many others, I wasn't being realistic enough. Since my ADHD diagnosis, I have thrown resolu-tions out the window altogether because, to me, they often imply that you are not enough, you've been doing it all wrong, and you need to fix yourself. Goals are great but must be healthy, realistic, and incremental. You don't need a new year to create new goals; you can accomplish them on your terms and in your own time.

It was Valentine's Day 2020, and I was meeting up with my friends for brunch and a good catch-up. My friends and I were discussing New Year's resolutions and what bullshit they are. Nevertheless, we were all still feeling victimized by them to some degree, working on goals with varying levels of success. I *was* spending less time on social media because I had no freaking time thanks to work, though unbeknownst to me, this would change in just one month due to the lockdown. Anyway, I had set my sights on something not completely surprising. I wanted to run a marathon. Though an avid runner, I had never done one. Okay, I lied: I watched the *Lord of the Rings* trilogy in its entirety in one single day once. Does that count?

To make matters worse, I publicly announced on Facebook that I was planning on running a marathon, with friends and family showing support through multiple heart emojis and "YOU GOT THIS!" in all caps in the comments. There was no backing down now, but could I complete it? I had a basic understanding of marathons, but it's safe to say that we all know that training involves more than running back and forth in your backyard with a frisbee and your dog. A marathon involves running 3-5 times a week, but I had been running less in 2018 and 2019. I thought I could handle a marathon out of the blue, but I was overwhelmed, realizing that my self-expectations were unrealistic. Then, the pandemic hit, and the marathon was canceled. Maybe it was luck or divine intervention, but I wasn't exactly upset when I learned it wouldn't happen. At least with lockdown, I could do the marathons I knew I had gotten good at: the ones on Netflix.

Self-expectations can be our biggest downfall and are hard to manage; however, by creating realistic ones attuned to our abilities and circumstances, they can set us up for success and improve how to deal with this thing called life. When it comes to creating realistic goals, there are a few tips to ensure they are more achievable such as:

- **Have a positive conversation with yourself.**
  Negative self-talk can creep in when trying to focus
  on our expectations. It's our way as overthinkers to
  convince ourselves to quit. Don't listen to your
  stupid brain; shift the perspective with positive
  self-talk. Consider using the power of affirmations
  by chanting them in your head or out loud. In
  every sports movie, the player always has a
  positive self-talk moment, haha, so why can't you?
  Or just put on *Eye of the Tiger*, pretend you're in
  Rocky 3, and "mind over matter" the shit out of
  whatever anxiety and fear you're feeling. (Fun
  survey pause: How many more times do you think
  I will evoke *Rocky* movies in this book?!)
- **Look at how far you've come and not how far you
  haven't.** You can get frustrated with not meeting
  your expectations, but you've achieved a lot
  already. So many people don't even bother doing
  anything for personal development or progress, yet
  you consciously try to be the opposite. Recalling a
  few things you have accomplished can keep you
  passionately within perspective.
- **Know that time IS on your side.** We can develop
  the "all or nothing" mindset when setting
  expectations, making us give up quickly. I should
  know. This is a classic trait of many ADHDers like
  myself. BUT. Rome wasn't built in a day; anything
  worthwhile involves patience and grit. Setbacks
  happen. If anything, we should always anticipate
  setbacks. It's ok to push back a deadline, as pushing
  yourself harder can lead to insufficient rest and
  leisure time, only stunting your progress. Being
  realistic means being flexible, too, and you have
  much more time than you realize.

- **Map it out.** What's usually the first thing you do before you go traveling? Make an itinerary or leave a turd on your boss's chair. The point is if you intend to reach expectations, creating a timeline or map with milestones can make it easier. Get a calendar and annotate the shit out of it. Trust me, getting organized will save you a headache.
- **It's okay to quit.** You may hyper-fixate on something you've never done, like "get a promotion." However, if that means working overtime every night and licking everyone's ass to get it, then is it really worth it? Part of setting self-expectations is the process, and sometimes, it's worth pursuing a different path entirely.
- **Confidence is key.** Gaining confidence comes with many perks, including adaptability when facing new challenges. You understand your limits and boundaries but are unafraid to seek help. If you are confident about what you can achieve, chances are, you'll fucking do it.
- **Be specific.** My biggest issue when it came to my own self-expectations was that they needed to be more specific. Run a fucking marathon? How did I intend to do that? Did I think I could magically do it because I used to run 3-7 miles in the woods regularly? A marathon is 26.2 effin' miles, through streets, with no control over a possible "freak" heat wave occurring in May (thank you, climate change). You need to hone in on what you want with great detail. What steps do you need to take? How much time do you need? And however much time you think you need as an ADHDer, double, nay, triple it. Do you need help doing it? Take a

moment to quiz yourself and fine-tune precisely
how you imagine things.

All that time in lockdown had a remarkable effect on me.
After I got bored of watching shit TV shows, I focused my
attention on YouTube. The cool thing about entering
keywords on YouTube is that it promotes videos you might
enjoy. It seems to get it mostly right, though once, when I
looked up crazy dog videos, the algorithm somehow recom-
mended hidden camera menopausal meltdown clips. I
observed, learned from my misperceptions, took notes, and
developed a detailed plan. And when I didn't hit my milestones — because, let's face it, all the sparkly planners, to-do
lists, and notes in the world won't always work for an overthinker, especially one with ADHD — I used positive self-talk
to reignite my passion and perspective. My confidence flour-
ished as I reached even the smallest of goals, from running
once to twice a week to five times as I had done for many
years. Both my body and my mind remembered what that
was like. As my confidence grew, I *knew* that the marathon
was achievable, and once I got the opportunity, I could sign
up for one after the pandemic.

Ultimately, I never registered because I decided that since
I had never liked running with other people, why would I
want to inflict that torture on myself? What was I trying to
prove? Many of my friends ran 5 and 10-K races all the time
and were constantly trying to get me to do one with them.
The thing is, thinking I wanted to do a marathon was actually
part of my masking. What I mean by that is that as a classic
ADHD people pleaser, I was constantly trying to fit in,
whether I realized it or not, and this behavior was exhausting.
I trained, got back in shape, and broke a personal record,
which was good enough for me. I knew I had the willpower,
determination, stamina, and fitness to complete the

marathon. Still, I had nothing to prove to anyone but myself, and I knew I could do it without actually doing it … in public … with a thousand other people. The lockdown gave me time to reflect on my self-expectations, as it did for many of us. With all that time stuck at home, I took a step back, learned to become more realistic, and set self-expectations based on that.

Expectations set the tone for how we approach a situation or outcome. Realistic expectations involve understanding what is likely to happen based on current circumstances and available resources. They are not specific objectives but rather a general mindset. My stint in lockdown taught me that I needed to make the best of my situation and backyard if I wanted to run a marathon. I had initially expected that I would succeed in the marathon back in 2020 with ease because of my athletic background, but the reality was that I was less conditioned than I used to be. With realistic expectations, we can recognize that achieving anything will take time and that progress is not strictly linear. Progress is flexible, and we can get shit done on our terms and in our own time. It's about how we think we can approach an outcome or situation, understanding what can happen based on our available resources and circumstances. Let's say I wanted to compete in a pie-eating competition; I loved eating pies, so I may have the self-expectation that I could win if I joined. However, to be more realistic in this approach, I would have to consider external factors like time constraints or limitations in my skills. Could I really eat so many pies? Can I afford to eat so many pies? (The answer to both those questions is no.)

This is where setting goals can come in. We all understand what a goal is. A goal is more or less an outcome we desire due to our ambitions and efforts. Goals are measurable and specific and give us a clear direction and focus. We have experienced setting goals throughout life: passing an exam, cooking an exquisite meal, trying to parallel park without somehow ending up floating down a river. Goals are challenging, for sure, but that's why they're fucking goals. Goals are also attainable, provided we are realistic about them. So, why is it hard to set realistic goals?

There are a myriad of reasons why setting a realistic goal is challenging. Sometimes, it's a lack of self-awareness. We need a clearer understanding of our strengths or limitations. We may be afraid to fail, so we don't even try. We need more support or resources to achieve the intended goal. A lack of motivation is another common culprit, leading to procrastination instead of taking action.

No matter the challenges, setting goals doesn't have to be so daunting. If I asked you where you see yourself in one year, five or ten years from now, that might be scary, and I don't subscribe to that "nailing down a precise time" point of view. But having *mini* goals might not be nearly as terrifying if you are realistic. Some possible side effects of setting *realistic* goals include:

- **Establishing a clear direction.** Imagine you wanted to start a business selling silly dog costumes. To do that, you should set a realistic goal of developing a business plan and figuring out how to secure funding. Direction and drive are two sides of the same coin, and when you know what you want, you can throw your passion in to get there.
- **Motivating yourself.** If you want to get fitter, maybe aiming for a trimmer waistline, a lower resting heart rate, or just more energy overall after three months instead of a "LOSE 10 lbs. IN A MONTH" mindset is more realistic to keep you motivated and give you a target to work on. Each time you reach a goal, you are further motivated to complete the next one. Sometimes a bunch of mini-

goals are way more effective than one big-ass overarching goal.

- **Witnessing progress.** If you were going to run a 5k race in six months, you could measure your progress and track your success effectively if you planned to run weekly. You could see what was working and what was not. I dare you to set goals that test your abilities so you can see your progress. But this only works if you try. If you don't try, you'll never know. I just said this, but it bears repeating for the ADHDers in particular who weren't paying attention the first time I said it several paragraphs back in this very chapter: so many ADHDers like me tend to have an "all or nothing" mindset, and this sets us up for self-sabotage from the start if we aren't willing to try something because we don't believe the end result will embody our perception of perfection. Remember that key takeaway from Chapter 3? The one about embracing uncertainty? Yeah, that one. Do that *and* learn to privilege putting something out there that feels potentially "mediocre" over the ultimate failure of untapped potential due to analysis paralysis, and you'll be golden.
- **Build confidence.** Talking in public is scary, but let's assume you set a goal to practice communicating daily by posting a reel a day because you want to grow your Instagram community. As each day passes and you stick to it, you will likely feel more capable and less inhibited and intimidated. It can help you overcome that fear of being on camera as your authentic self and build confidence and self-esteem.

- **Become more accountable.** Setting goals lets you see what's wrong and decide what to do. If you are not reaching the goals you select, you can address the problem and try to find a solution by setting mini-goals that will help you achieve the larger goal. Some of us just need more time to complete tasks. Some of us need to take baby steps. Body doubling or hiring a coach also helps many people who struggle with this.
- **Take control of your life.** Many of us work and work, and when you hit your 30s, 40s, and beyond, BOOM, if you're burned out, you may feel exhausted and have no idea what to do next in life. Setting goals turns off the autopilot we've been using to navigate and think about what we want. I wanted to be less stressed and have positive financial momentum in my life. My job as a professor was very fulfilling and stimulating in many ways, but ultimately, the cons outweighed the pros. I was stressed around the clock, and my salary barely budged each year as the cost of living rose faster than my pay. It was frightening as fuck, but I had to get control of my life. I quit that job, and I have never looked back. I am now living life and getting shit done on my terms. I'm not rolling in the dough yet (unless you mean cookie dough), but my life is already so much richer mentally. And the money part? Well, that's coming. Can you say "manifesting?"
- **Reach your fullest potential.** It's one of the best reasons, if not THE reason. Setting goals is the solution if you are tired of the what-ifs and the maybes. Without goals, we tend to fall into default mode, but with goals, we have things to work

towards. I remember a kid in school who used to sell candy to other kids on the playground. Each time he hit record sales for the week, he would aim to beat the number the week after. That kid was Elon Musk. Okay, that's total bullshit, LOL, it wasn't, but my point is this: if the only person you compete with is yourself, then you can set the terms and have fun succeeding in your way and in your own time. One of my primary life goals is financial freedom by age 55. This goal is realistic, gives me plenty of time, and leaves plenty of room for fucking up and starting over, as well as trying something new if I want to. The key? KNOW THY SELF.

Okay, it's time for another true story. Back in college, which was tough because we didn't have Wikipedia and had to practically live in the library, I had a roommate named Christina. Christina and I loved to party and spent so much time at social gatherings our first two years that we barely made it to class. When we did attend, we often sat in the very back because we could try to sleep off our hangovers in relative obscurity. My friends partied a lot, too, but Christina and I were next-level partiers. Some of our friends were worried, but even when they tried an "intervention," we turned it into a party. Shit hit the fan, though, when Christina and I both learned some hard truths. I'll spare you all the boring details of mine, but suffice it to say that academic mediocrity wasn't as fun as it seemed for me. I was a closet perfectionist who pretended not to give a shit and who had no clue that I had ADHD. But I did want to succeed. Had I known I had ADHD all along, that would have explained a lot, and maybe I could have gotten the help I needed. But ADHD wasn't really a thing back then. It was still called ADD, was highly stigmatized, considered a behavioral issue that afflicted only six-year-old boys, and, well, we didn't know that much about it. Basically, I was on a steady path to depression, anxiety, substance abuse, and probably dropping out or flunking out of college if I did not get my shit together. As for Christina, she would have to retake her organic chemistry course if she failed her next exam. Christina took a moment to reflect on where she was in life. Did she want a biology degree, or did she want to move back in with her parents?

I, too, thought about what it would be like to move back home. It's a tough decision if you ask me. For a split second, I considered the perks of moving back in with my parents – pursuing my true passion in life, and becoming a professional hide-and-seeker – after all, I'd spent most of my life up to that point hiding from my problems by overthinking everything – might as well put those skills to good use! But after that split second passed, I (and Christina) wisely chose the student route. Christina crafted a study schedule and went to all her classes completely sober. I did the same and read through my lecture notes every night. My entire bedroom wall was filled with Post-it notes like something from CSI. Well, when it came to her next big exam, she passed with flying colors and subsequently got her degree. And I figured out exactly what I would need to do, change, and sacrifice to graduate with a 3.0 and finish college on time. And you know what? I did it. In retrospect, that goal was exceptionally lofty and would not have been realistic for other students. But I achieved it to the letter (mostly) because I did not simply imagine these goals in a vacuum. I reimagined the next several years of my life, set my intentions, and researched the required changes. that. shit. happen.

We had the brains and capabilities to succeed yet went into default mode through all the partying and none of the learning. Thankfully, Christina and I buckled down and set realistic goals before it was too late. And you can, too!

Before you set a realistic goal, ask yourself:

- Do I want/need direction in my life?
- Do I want/need to find a sense of purpose?
- Do I want/need to realize my potential?

I mean, I have learned through way more trial and even more error than I care to admit that although I do not like the thought of structure, my ADHD ass *needs* routine. So the simple answer to the above questions for most people is "holy fuck, yes!" as it has been for eons and eons. Now, take a moment to consider once again where you see yourself in one year, in five years, and ten years. As horrifying as it is to face your doomsday dream, what if it was the opposite? What if all worked out?

That's enough what-ifs; if we dwell on it anymore, we will turn into a sparkling sack of shit at midnight. Before setting important life-changing goals, you should expect to fail, but don't let yourself give up. It would help if you persevered with patience and persistence. Most importantly, DO NOT compare your journey with anyone else's. (For the record, I loathe the word "journey" and avoid it at all costs, but it felt annoyingly appropriate here.) Just because your neighbor is putting out elaborate Christmas decorations on the roof a month before you doesn't mean you also need to. They will have an enormous electricity bill anyway, and everyone else in the neighborhood secretly rolls their eyes at them as much as you. Enough messing around; let's get to it. We need to be SMART here. Yep, it is time for an awesome acronym: Specified, Measurable, Attainable, Relevant, and Time-bound. Woohoo!

There are many ways to set a goal, but the SMART

method is simple and adaptable to neurotypical and neurodivergent brains. The purpose is to keep the process simple; otherwise, you might need help. So, let's look at the steps necessary:

- **1 Specified.** First, you have to define what you want. What do you hope to accomplish? What steps are needed? Are you the only one responsible for this? Why is the goal important to you? You can't simply want to read a book once a week, or even once a month, for no reason. You can be general with some stuff, but goals won't feel like goals if they are too vague.

- **2 Measurable.** The goal must be measurable; otherwise, you can't track the progress you make and stay motivated. Looking at our progress reinforces focus, helps us meet deadlines, and, most importantly, drives us to reach our goals. If you were starting a blog about unique scented candles such as "dirty hippie deluxe" or "pitbull fartastic," you might measure your success by how many views your site got, comments, or shares. You choose how you want to measure.

- **3 Attainable.** It should be within your abilities, skills, and means to reach your intended goal or goals. So, being realistic here is vital. Do you need money for it, and if so, do you have enough? If you want to gain more followers on your TikTok, are you willing to engage with people consistently and positively? Are you willing to show up? I have historically sucked at social media, but with my @sarcrasstic.self.care account on Instagram, I wanted to build an engaging and meaningful community. My growth was prolonged at first because I would post randomly and sporadically, and then not engage if anyone commented, and sometimes even go MIA for a week or two at the beginning. I was uncomfortable putting myself out there and had not yet gotten my ADHD diagnosis. But the second I learned I had ADHD, it was on. The community on Instagram was the whole reason how I started realizing that this had been my issue all along and subsequently sought a diagnosis. I wanted to pay it forward by sharing my lived experiences and humor in hopes of helping others who are late-diagnosed like me not feel so alone. It was hard. And it's still hard at times. But, sometimes, setting a goal for something a little out of our comfort zone can challenge us to focus harder. The old adage "Where there's a will, there's a way" goes a long way if your will is strong enough. If you're stubborn as hell like me, chances are almost anything you set your mind to is attainable in time.

- **4 Relevant.** Does your goal relate to your overall life objectives? Does it align with your values and vision? Are you the right person for this goal? Are you willing to make some sacrifices to make this goal a reality? If you want something you've never had, you're likely going to have to do shit you've never done before. And, trust me, I get it. That's scary. But once again, it's all about being realistic and knowing yourself.
- **5 Timely.** In theory, a goal should have some semblance of an end date; otherwise, what are you working towards? As a recovering overthinker, time is something we spend too much time on. With a goal, we can look at how much time we

realistically may need to reach it and what we hope to achieve to get there. Trying to improve and progress in anything takes time, but without goals, it will probably not happen as efficiently as you'd like. Setting an end doesn't have to be so daunting. Again, be realistic, know yourself, and set a deadline with some natural accountability if you need more time. Publicly post on your socials so others know what you're up to unless it's a marathon you don't really want to run in the first place. I find that public accountability is a great way to motivate myself and spark conversations that enlist my community to help keep me on track. You don't have to be mega-specific with time, but ultimately, you do need to choose some sort of deadline for yourself.

Setting a goal is a lifetime achievement for us over-thinkers. We hate the word. Pro tip: if you detest the word "goal," then replace it with whatever works for you: your hella hopes, your dare to dreams, your diabolical desires, your crazy life campaigns. We overthinkers tend to shy away from goals. So many of us have analysis paralysis, and I, personally and historically, suffer from imposter syndrome. I know, first and foremost, that *you are enough.* Sometimes phrases like that are a little cheesy for my darker, edgier, punk-ass personality, but it's true. I have often gotten so over-whelmed by available choices that I couldn't make any deci-sion at all. We overthinkers want everything figured out before we start; if not, we see no point in trying. I used to be like this. The worst thing is we can end up overthinking so much about taking control of our lives that we get stuck in panic mode and fall victim to massive anxiety attacks. This has happened to me more times than I care to confess. I've had panic attacks just thinking about panic attacks. So, what do you do when overthinking attacks like this? I have not had a severe panic attack in years, thankfully, and the next chapter will explain why.

————

Key takeaway: Set realistic goals and expectations for yourself. Just remember, the sky's not the limit. The finish line in the race against yourself is the same, no matter your pace.

CHAPTER FIVE

PRESSING PAUSE ON THE
PANIC BUTTON:
DISARMING ANXIETY BOMBS BEFORE THEY
EXPLODE

"I CAME. I saw. I had anxiety. So I left."
— Unknown

I used to overthink often, and sometimes, it would evolve into an anxiety attack. These would appear out of nowhere, and I would have no idea what was happening. It seemed like these moments of paralyzing anxiety would spring from out of the blue sometimes. You could be putting the star on your Christmas tree and have an attack. You could be having your third venti mocha latte with extra whip and have one. You could have an attack as you cross the street, and the signal turns red before you make it across. Sometimes, it can seem like anything and everything can set us off, yet we may have no idea what the hell it is.

In the '90s and '00s, there wasn't a surplus of movies related to my feelings and experiences with anxiety and over-thinking that I felt I could connect to. I may be wrong here, and you can tell me I am wrong. Still, as we entered the digital age with the internet, it helped significantly raise awareness about mental health, with many people openly talking about their experiences. More movies have come out to reflect this. You may wonder why this is important. A good movie is a focal reference point to a moment in time, but it can also make us feel like we are not the only ones going full-blown crazy. When *The Matrix* came out in 1999, people were terrified that robots would take over, and *The Truman Show* made us paranoid about cameras and peeping toms. These movies raised questions but also gave us insight. What I wanted, though, was a movie where someone overthinks, like me and many others, because we exist, goddamn it!

When *Silver Linings Playbook* came out in 2012, I thought it was just another cash cow rom-com. I am willing to admit now that I was maybe *somewhat* wrong. As much as I hate to say it, this film surprised me because it explored mental health in a more relatable and realistic way than it could have. There was one particular scene that I appreciated. Pat, played by Bradley Cooper (no matter what you think of him, he was instantly delicious to me the moment I heard him speaking fluent French), turns up to a formal dinner party dressed in a sports jersey instead of something more sophisticated. As he stood at the front door, Pat decided he was underdressed and began to leave, only for his best friend to open the door and catch him in time, telling him he looked fine. Pat wanted to wear the jersey because he liked it, but he got so overwhelmed that he was ready to give it all up and go home instead. I'm all about the dark European art films that leave everything hanging and have no happy ending, no resolution. But whatever. Sure, this movie has the typical Hollywood ending (in which everything is perfect or slightly resolved), but don't we all deserve that too? Shouldn't there be a light at the end of the tunnel for anyone who experiences panic attacks caused by overthinking?

An anxiety or panic attack is a present moment of obsessive thoughts or spiraling worry that manifests suddenly, often due to a trigger. If you ever felt a rapid stream of negative thoughts flooding your mind so much that you got overwhelmed, felt like you were having a heart attack, and felt paralyzed or frozen, you definitely experienced one. And they are brutal. Imagine that you won the lottery. You want to celebrate your luck with family and friends, but then suddenly, you ask yourself whether you should tell anyone for fear that you are more likely to get robbed. Loads of negative thoughts come flying in, and suddenly, you start panicking. In 2019, one lottery winner dressed in a Scream costume to hide his identity when he collected his winnings (the photos online are hilarious, at least). Like Ghostface, I wanted to hide my identity behind a mask, especially on one occasion.

The first date after a significant time being single is scary. The first date after getting a divorce is a million times worse. I have been through it, and so many of my friends have as well. I remember when my friend Heather decided to go on a date years ago after her divorce. She told me this:

"In hindsight, maybe I should have called it off, as my anxiety levels were already pretty high before I even reached the café. As I stood in front of the door, I couldn't physically enter." (HEY! Just like Pat from the movie!)

Heather continued: "I was panicking and second-guessing if this was the right decision. Thoughts flooded in like, what if he didn't like what I was wearing? What if I get rejected? What if I say something wrong?"

I interrupted right there (as we ADHDers do) to commiserate and remind her that for me, ADHD dictates that I am the queen of oversharing and blurting out inappropriate shit, and so I completely empathized with the "What if I say something wrong?" bit.

Heather also wondered at the moment: "What if I still have some emotional baggage? What if he knows my ex?"

She told me she wanted to turn around and head home and was just about to do so until he spotted her. So she put on a fake smile and walked in. As they sat together, Heather noticed she wasn't being her usual upbeat self. Each time this guy asked her something, she would barely reply. It was like he was on a date with a mannequin. She was worried about saying the wrong thing more than simply being herself.

So, Heather's first date ended after maybe 45 minutes, and she felt so useless. She said this guy was awesome. She felt like she had totally messed it up. The anxiety overshadowed her when she wanted to be at her best. Then, she got a text later in the evening from the awesome guy she thought she had screwed up her date with. At this point, she had had two glasses of red wine and thought, "screw it, just tell him the truth!" Now, usually, decisions involving alcohol are not good, but then many babies probably wouldn't have been born had it not been for them. The bad alcohol-induced decisions, that is. He replied right back, telling her not to worry and that he, too, was recently divorced and feeling a bit shy about getting back out there. Well, at least they had something in common.

I have learned so much about how overthinking has affected my past relationships and friendships that I have needlessly worried about my present and future ones. Some of the ways overthinking has impacted my relationships include:

- **Communicating poorly.** I should have told my partner about my overthinking so we could work together on agreed-upon boundaries.
- **Trying to mind-read.** I often tried to figure out what my partner was thinking and occasionally jumped to conclusions. At times, I should have

asked for clarification or reassurance instead of assuming the worst.

- **Needing to trust more.** Whenever I had trust issues, I should have worked on them with my partner through open communication. The stronger the trust, the less overthinking as a result.
- **Respecting private space more.**
- A bit of space is always good, but as an overthinker, you might assume your partner is up to something nefarious outside, like trying to take over the world. No, wait, that's me. Give them space. Let them have fun without you.

It's tough enough dealing with overthinking on our own, let alone having a partner have to deal with our shit, too. For so long, I thought I was the only one, and for too long, my overthinking contributed to my developing anxiety. Over-thinking keeps our minds aroused and hyperactive, meaning we struggle to sleep and become even more anxious. Then, sometimes, out of the blue, we feel something so mentally overwhelming that it affects us physically. Enter once more the anxiety or panic attack, and symptoms can peak within 10 minutes after it suddenly comes. Doctors typically diagnose a panic or anxiety attack by looking for at least four of the following telltale signs:

- Sweating
- Trembling
- Shortness of breath
- A choking sensation
- Chest pain and/or nausea
- Dizziness
- Fear of losing your mind
- Feeling hot or cold

- Numbness or tingling
- A racing heart (heart palpitations)
- Feeling unusually detached from yourself

I have experienced multiple panic attacks over the years, and they were frankly frightening at first. Yep, they were fucking awful. One of the worst ones I can recall was when everything was falling apart, or at least it felt like it. Back when I was a student, I had this big assignment to finish; at the same time, I was in a complicated relationship and was trying to keep my shitty bartending job. Anyway, I was at work, and a drunk girl got into a fight with another equally drunk girl, and fists started flying. I tried to break up the fight but got hurt in the process, and the next thing I remember, I couldn't breathe. I got heart palpitations and chest pains and started sweating my ass off, and I had no idea what was going on. After fifteen minutes, I felt better. Maybe not 100%, but definitely better. "I was the bartender serving them drinks; I didn't deserve this!" I kept thinking to myself. After that awful experience, I quit my job. It was good, in a way. I could focus on school and my boyfriend, though with no job, I had to live off ramen. I thought I was ok until after I finished my last exam, and my friends wanted to go to a bar to celebrate. As we stepped into the bar, I became overly anxious, looking around frantically in case I saw any stupid and exceptionally strong drunk girls and an anxiety attack came out of nowhere.

For so long, I had no idea what was going on. But just like the Bradley Cooper movie, there was a silver lining (oh come on, admit it, you saw it coming): finding the motivation to prioritize self-care and build resilience. I eventually went to the doctor and told her what I had experienced, and I learned it was an anxiety attack. You'd think they could give it a more subtle, less scary name than that, maybe like a worry whirlwind or stress salsa. My anxiety attack was likely triggered by a reminder of the traumatic bar experience, and it took me a long time until I could enter a bar again. But I have been triggered because of high levels of stress, too, due to school, work, and relationship stress. So many different things can trigger anxiety attacks, such as:

- **Stress.** From my experience, you can get super stressed by work, school, relationships, or other life events. Overwhelming or chronic stress can push the body and mind into a state of heightened anxiety, potentially leading to an anxiety attack.
- **Caffeine.** Some of us get stressed from not having coffee in the morning, but in rare instances, too much coffee can also lead to an attack by increasing your heart rate. Know your limits, people.
- **Phobias.** Phobias are intense and irrational fears of specific objects, situations, or activities. When confronted with a phobia, you can get triggered, which leads to an anxiety attack. If you were afraid to fly, getting on a plane would be terrifying.
- **Major life transitions.** Significant life changes (such as moving to a new place, starting a new job, having kids, going through a divorce, or, say, quitting a life-long career and writing a book about your overthinking brain) may stress you out so much that it triggers anxiety attacks. Transitions in life often involve uncertainty, loss, or the need to adapt to new circumstances, making you anxious enough to have an attack.
- **Health concerns.** Ever heard of hypochondria? Also known as illness anxiety disorder, it is the condition where someone constantly worries about

their health, and it can also sometimes lead to an attack.

- **Arguments or conflict.** An intense argument or conflict is tricky as you need to find a solution with your spouse, partner, colleague, or friend, which can give you more anxiety because you feel you don't have control over the situation.
- **Social situations**. Sometimes, we feel uncomfortable in social situations. I know I do. But sometimes, we get completely overwhelmed when there is so much noise or too many people that it can trigger an anxiety attack. Since my ADHD diagnosis, I have learned that both introversion and sensory overload are a thing.

Experiencing an overthinking attack or, worse, a physical anxiety panic attack is a horrific experience, but here's your silver lining playbook of coping mechanisms. Every person is different, and some techniques will work better than others. Before I reveal the weird, unconventional method that worked for me, I want to highlight some other ways, such as:

- **Avoid triggers altogether.** In some ways, it is one of the most straightforward techniques. I know from experience that this is not always possible. I have had panic attacks with no apparent trigger. But, if you are aware of what situations or environments have the potential to provoke your anxiety, you will be more successful at avoiding them, thereby reducing the chances of having an anxiety attack. Then again, you may have to face them at some point in life, like realizing you're out of coffee on a Monday morning. Talk about a perfect recipe for an anxiety attack - caffeine withdrawal and a long day ahead, but sometimes you gotta face that shit head-on and power through if you can.

- **Take intentional, timed deep breaths.** When you have an attack, you may hyperventilate; however, shifting to deep, long breaths for four seconds can help minimize hyperventilating and help reduce the effects.

- **Recognize that it's anxiety.** The first and even second and third time I had a severe panic attack - and I know people can relate to this - I thought I was having a heart attack. Yep. I truly believed I was dying at that moment, and it was scary. When panic attack symptoms like a racing heart, cold sweats, and tingling and numbing in your left arm down to your fingertips mimic those of a heart attack, who wouldn't think this? When you feel like you are having an anxiety attack and become self-conscious about the experience, remind yourself that it's only temporary and will pass soon. This can stop you from thinking that you are about to die (which fuels your anxiety further) and help you remember it's only a short-lived moment.

- **Learn and utilize grounding techniques.** When you feel as though you are about to have an anxiety attack, try to engage your senses with your immediate surroundings. Look for five things you can see: four things you can touch, three things you can hear, two things you can smell, and one thing you can taste. (Hernandez-Santana 2022) This reasonably simple exercise can put all your attention on something present instead of your anxious thoughts.

- **Repeat a mantra.** I won't lie: I didn't use to be the biggest fan of mantras; however, thinking to yourself, "This will pass," or "Shut the fuck up, it's not real," may just be the thing that helps prevent you from having a full-blown meltdown.

Overthinking too much may lead to anxiety, which may lead to an attack, but remember that you are so much more than your thoughts. Your thoughts don't dictate your life, nor should they encourage you how to live your life. What you perceive is only sometimes the reality unless you live in Neverland. I have explored and tried every method out there, including the ones I listed, but I came up with my own unique remedy, though the grounding technique heavily influenced it.

When I felt overwhelmed to the point that I was about to have an anxiety attack, I would look around me and find two unrelated objects. Depending on where I am at that moment, it could be anything. So, let's say I am at a bar and spot a bright pink handbag and a cocktail umbrella. Next, I want to find one word that describes a feeling; I will say embarrassed in this context. Create a ridiculous scenario involving both objects and the feeling you chose. For example:

- Maybe the pink handbag was embarrassed that the cocktail umbrella couldn't quite fit inside.
- Maybe the cocktail umbrella was embarrassed that the pink handbag was full of stolen pens and felt inferior.
- Maybe the pink handbag opened, and the cocktail umbrella was embarrassed to find his best friend, the cocktail napkin, there.

We add more details to the story to make it even funnier and ridiculous. So, I will pick the third one:

- Cocktail Umbrella got furious with his best friend and tried to prick the cocktail napkin, only for the pink handbag to quickly zip up.
- Cocktail Umbrella was shocked to see Cocktail Napkin, but there was enough room for a cocktail party.
- Pink Handbag quickly zipped up her front and unzipped her back pouch for Cocktail Umbrella.

I know. Some spicy innuendos in there, but they sure make things exciting and sexy, too! Try this simple yet effective storytelling trick the next time you feel anxious. Heck, you could even try it now. And if you want to take it a step further, name the objects. Cary the Cocktail Umbrella. Nico the Napkin. Patricia Purse. Etc. It seems counterintuitive, but many things in life are like this. Taking breaks helps you study, and embracing failures enables you to succeed more. Incorporating humor can shift your perspective, give a temporary distraction, and help lighten the intensity of the anxiety experience at hand.

If you need help with creativity and can't come up with a story based on your surroundings, there is another excellent suggestion. Anytime I feel like I am heading toward a breakdown, I unwind by watching a funny movie or comedy show. It is usually the first thing I put on after a long-ass day working. Laughter is the best medicine, right? I mean, it's addictive. It feels so good. There are many comedians out there who conquered their anxiety and depression by performing stand-up comedy. They found a silver lining. I spent each day after work watching something funny and making a diet of it, and it helped to decrease my anxiety, as having a good chuckle will reduce stress hormones instantly. As we laugh, we also increase our oxygen intake, allowing our muscles to relax and reducing anxiety even further. Of course, it's hard to laugh when you are in the midst of an actual anxiety attack, but this is where a distraction can come in. Try to think about something funny by looking around you or recall a hilarious joke you heard before. Watching a good comedy show or film helps me fully unwind. Humor is subjective, but depending on your taste, some universally favorite comedies include:

- Old-school American shows like *I Love Lucy, Good Times, The Jeffersons,* or *Three's Company*
- American series like *Seinfeld, Curb Your Enthusiasm,* and *How I Met Your Mother*
- Older British series like *The Young Ones, Monty Python,* and *Absolutely Fabulous*
- Films like *Bridesmaids, Scary Movie, Bad Teacher* & *Mean Girls*
- Anything involving Harold and Kumar
- Anything with Jim Carrey
- Or even *The Room* (a cult classic that is so bad it's good)
- Re-runs of sketch comedy shows like *SNL, In Living Color, Key and Peele,* and *SCTV*

At some point, though, you may have watched every comedy movie and series, so better yet, attend a comedy show (just don't sit at the front unless you want an immediate anxiety attack when the performer asks for your name).

No matter what trick, technique, or tip helps you prevent or overcome an attack, you have to find that silver lining, or in other words, find what works for you and use it more. When you have an attack, you have to remember that you are not freaking dying, and by diverting your attention, you can reduce the effect of it. One of the more recent times I can recall having a massive anxiety attack or feeling like I was about to have one was on the underground during rush hour in London in the fall of 2021 (which is a terrible idea, and I would rather travel by cow). I was in too much of a rush, but as more and more people crammed in, I felt anxious. I took a moment to look around me and noticed a dog and a carrot. I thought about how excited the dog could be to see the carrot if it could play with it. I then thought maybe the dog would take the carrot to the park to show off to his other dog friends and make them jealous. Who hasn't been jealous over a carrot, right? I somehow managed to avert my attack by using my mind to make up a silly story instead.

Back to the silver lining, we can find it in so many things in life. We can find a job we absolutely hate and make a best friend. The degree we worked so hard to find and never got a job in might teach us some killer skills for a career in a different field. I would be remiss if I did not acknowledge that working in academia as a professor offered me countless opportunities for travel, activism, public speaking, honing the latest tech skills, attending writing workshops, you name it. I learned so much while I taught others, and I don't take that for granted! Thank goodness my former workplace and colleagues were not toxic. And yet, we can find that an unhealthy relationship makes us more open and honest in the ones that follow. The same can be said for dealing with over-thinking and anxiety attacks. There is usually a silver lining if you open your eyes enough or listen closely enough.

This shift in mindset is drastically beneficial because it develops a sense of self-awareness. It shows us that we don't need to be victims constantly and that instead of stressing and worrying, we can learn to grow once we master our minds. And it's okay if some days you don't feel like your mind's master. It's that self-awareness that is key.

The next chapter focuses on … hear me out nay-sayers … the growth mindset, where challenges become opportunities, even for ADHDers. Embracing what we fear will ultimately help us get what we want.

———

Key takeaway: Learn how to manage your overthinking and anxiety attacks in ways that work for you.

 **INTERMISSION**

Wait, what? You're still here?! Maybe you've ADHD hyper-focused your way through the first half of this book without coming up for air. Or perhaps you read just a paragraph before bed each night and had to re-read it because your ADHD is the inattentive "can't focus at all" type, waking suddenly with this book on your head (if you bought a hard copy) only to realize you'd fallen asleep mid-sentence and now the page where you left off is saturated with drool. Regardless, *I am so honored you are here!*

Well, this is the perfect moment for all those ADHDers, in particular, out there to get off your butts and use the bathroom (or if you're British, the loo), eat a sandwich, drink a glass of water, or all of the above. And while I've got you here before you sink your beautiful teeth into the next chapter, or a sandwich, quick favor!

If you've been laughing along with me and believe this book is helping you feel less alone, feel seen and understood, and is giving you some unconventional yet absolutely realistic strategies for easing your anxiety with a laugh, consider leaving a positive review on the platform where you purchased it.

Your voice matters. And our stories matter. If we don't tell them, who will? People give a shit about what you think! Help a punk sister out by saying a few words about how this book impacted you. Detailed reviews help potential readers decide whether this book is for them.

I invite you to help me help others embrace their radically authentic selves and calm their anxious, overthinking brains, one obnoxious cackle at a time.

I appreciate you!
Now, let's get back to it.

CHAPTER SIX

NURTURING YOUR NEUROSIS: HOW TO TRANSFORM ANXIOUS ENERGY INTO PERSONAL GROWTH

"IN THE MIDDLE of every difficulty lies opportunity."
– Albert Einstein

I have a real passion for learning, and no, it's not because of my background in education. You are always young enough to learn something new. The other day, I realized it's impossible to tickle yourself (and a clear sign you spend too much time alone). It's useless information, but hey, it's still something. (We ADHDers are full of random knowledge!) Learning is a driving tool; it can empower us, give us potential, and help move our lives forward. It should come as no surprise, then, that I am a big fan of Ted Talks; they are so engaging, fascinating, and free to watch online. I would love to do a talk on "how to effectively use your middle finger daily" with a segment focused on how to slowly transition from saying hello straight to the middle finger. I wish I were born with more middle fingers sometimes. After binge-watching a few talks, I wondered how the speakers oozed confidence in front of so many people. It made me wonder, "How did they get successful?"

Success is relative. Success is subjective. For some, a successful person sets goals and achieves them. They are doers, not thinkers (or overthinkers even). To some, a successful person feels fulfilled; to others, success is defined by their status or career. We often describe success in many ways, but author Maya Angelou put it best: "Success is liking yourself, liking what you do, and liking how you do it." No matter the definition, successful people tend to have willpower, drive, and passion, but above all else, they have a growth mindset. Yeah, yeah. I know. I used to cringe at all the "success salespeople" and the "growth mindset" pushers, but I have come around. So just hear me out because success and growth can still be on YOUR terms, and I know you want to grow and succeed. At least I hope you do. I've heard shrinking and failing really suck. But where was I? Oh, yes...

A growth mindset is a term used to describe people who believe that their success depends on their effort and time. They think they can improve in anything they set their mind to, often embracing challenges instead of shying away. Dr. Carol Dweck of Stanford University developed the concept first. Dr. Dweck's research and studies on motivation and student behavior led her to the revelation that people with this mindset were more successful than those with a fixed mindset. Dweck concluded that individuals with a growth mindset believed their abilities would improve through perseverance, dedication, and time.

In contrast, those with a fixed mindset thought they couldn't change their traits. For too long, I, too, had a fixed mindset. The following isn't meant as a jab at my ex-husband: He's a really good guy, but my fixed mindset kept me in a marriage that wasn't working for me for way too long. It also kept me from doing more with music in my life, leaving my last job, and getting to the point where I was far past burnout when I finally decided that something had to give.

Whenever friends would call to invite me to yoga classes, I would hesitate about joining because I thought I wouldn't like it. My ADHD ass loved to run through trails in the woods for hours with Public Enemy and Rage Against the Machine blaring in my earbuds, and the thought of doing something so slow and quiet while confined to a mat did not appeal to me, like, at all. When my daughter wanted me to do the bottle cap TikTok challenge, the one where you round-house-kick the cap off a bottle without knocking it over, I would worry about losing my balance and breaking my neck. I even hated making pumpkin pie for Thanksgiving dinner because I believed I could never be good at baking, so my then-husband always did it. When you have kids, a house, a full-time job, etc, you feel like you have no time to squeeze in anything else, and if you do, you assume you can't change anything, so you don't bother. You think that the classic adage "you can't teach an old dog new tricks" is your life motto. However, in my 40s, I put any shred of growth mindset I had on steroids, and it was the catalyst for the second part of my life. Once I stopped feeling like I was too old to change my life and started to believe that I was still very young, this new way of thinking spring-boarded me into a new world.

The fixed mindset is what I like to call the old way of thinking. Anyone with this mindset will avoid challenges, give up quickly before even trying, and sometimes feel intim-idated by the success of other people, which is likely because intelligence and talent are seen as something you are born with rather than something you can work on. The more significant issue with a fixed mindset is that it can lead to negative thinking. If you fail, you assume you aren't good or smart enough. I have an ADHD friend from a big family; his siblings often called him the "brainy one" since he frequently learned new skills, traveled the world, and constantly worked on "improving" himself. It's an ADHD stereotype that we get bored quickly and hop from one new project, interest, or hobby to the next, so it's no surprise that he came off as restless and eccentric to his family. Neither his parents nor his siblings had ever left the country or even strayed more than one or two states over from home when it came down to it. He tried to encourage them to travel and try new things, but he would be met with excuses on how they weren't "born smart and adventurous" like him. They didn't have the money to travel like him, even though his job didn't pay exceptionally well, and he saved and budgeted to afford his adventures and hobbies.

Having a fixed mindset means you are more likely to:

- Assume that intelligence and talent are static, meaning, they can't ever be changed
- Avoid any challenge because you are afraid of failure
- Ignore any form of feedback as you see it as criticism
- Feel threatened by the success of others
- Hide what you perceive as flaws because you are worried about being judged by others
- Believe putting in the effort is worthless, so you don't even freaking bother
- Give up quickly, like trying to assemble flat-packed furniture from IKEA

Luckily, you aren't born with *all* your intelligence, as fixed-minded folks might assume, but you also don't have to think you aren't smart precisely because of a fixed mindset. With a growth mindset, you believe in your intelligence and talents and that you can improve on them. With a growth mindset, you see setbacks and failures as stepping stones, a necessary part of the learning process.

Though mostly homeschooled in high school, when they were younger, my kids were lucky enough to have some teachers who never gave homework. They felt it was better if students finished their work in class since there were more readily available resources and support. Without the pressure of completing homework assignments, students could focus more on the learning process in class, and the teachers could concentrate on providing immediate feedback that helped them learn from their mistakes in real-time. Without giving homework, these teachers could create an environment that encourages students to become more responsible and take ownership of their learning, which is crucial to developing a growth mindset. The bottom line is screw homework for young kids, but there I go again with my digressing.

Having a growth mindset means you are more likely to:

- Place more focus, energy, and effort into learning
- Believe that efforts will lead to mastery
- Conceptualize failure as a sometimes necessary but temporary setback
- Embrace challenges, knowing they will lead to progress
- See feedback as vital and an opportunity to learn
- View the success of others as an inspiration
- Believe intelligence can be amplified
- Develop a love of lifelong learning

A fixed mindset, unfortunately, has more in common with overthinking than a growth mindset. It doesn't mean you can't cultivate a growth mindset; if anything, people tend to have traits from both mindsets. And ADHDers, unfortunately, can be more susceptible to getting caught up and stuck in fixed mindsets due to negative self-perceptions from a very young age. Researchers estimate that kids with ADHD get more than 20,000 negative or corrective messages from parents, teachers, and other adults by the time they are ten years old than their friends and siblings who do not have ADHD (Dodson, 2022; Jellinek, 2010).

"By the time children are 7 or 8 years of age, their self-esteem has huge holes, and their identity is often centered on not being smart or good enough," and "When we consider parenting children with ADHD, it's important to look beyond actions, executive functions, and what they are doing. It is deeply important to discover, uncover, and support who they are and who they are becoming" (Hoyle, 2023; Panepinto, 2019).

That said, if you wish to get the most out of life, having supportive friends and family can help you cultivate a growth mindset, which will likely help you reach your desired goals faster.

Watching Ted Talks, I get inspired by the speakers and the fact that they have a story to tell and do it with such confidence and clarity. I watch these talks and think, "Wow, this makes so much sense!" But at the same time, as much as I admire their success, as someone who used to have a more fixed mindset, I once saw my own failures as reasons not to bother trying to set goals. I also made the mistake of constantly comparing myself to others. Remember: YOU set the terms of your growth and success. Don't let others define it for you. As I watched more and more talks, though, I realized I was actually learning. You may listen to podcasts, watch documentaries on Netflix, or watch YouTube videos that educate you on different things, helping you grow (and maybe without even realizing it). The growth mindset doesn't happen overnight; nothing worthwhile does, and the first step is acknowledging the fixed "old way of thinking" mindset before learning to cultivate the growth "new way of thinking" mindset.

The fixed mindset is often fostered by overthinking and displays the following tendencies:

- **Overthinking (wow, really?!)**: Overthinking is often fueled by a fixed mindset. With a fixed mindset, you might assume your abilities and intelligence are fixed traits and that challenges and setbacks reflect your limitations. This results in worrying about making mistakes or not meeting your own or others' expectations.
- **Fear of Failure:** One of the most extensive drives of overthinking is a fear of failure, and people with a fixed mindset tend to see failure as a personal reflection of their skills and abilities. This results in never taking risks or trying new things because we want to avoid potential failures, thereby hindering our potential progress and growth.
- **Perfectionism:** As overthinkers, we want everything to be perfect. With a fixed mindset, you have an intense desire to come across as flawless and competent, making you also self-critical and over-analytical. This can prevent you from taking risks and learning from errors and cause you to ignore opportunities for growth.
- **Limited Perspective**: Overthinking usually leads to a vicious cycle of negative self-talk and repetitive thoughts. We end up with a limited perspective that prevents us from developing a growth mindset, quashing creativity, assertiveness, and the ability to consider alternative solutions. In sum, it keeps us from being effective problem solvers.

I used to have a fixed mindset in many ways; I never knew I had one until I watched a Ted Talk by Dr. Carol

Dweck (yes, the one-and-the-same badass Stanford professor I cited at the beginning of this chapter) on "the power of believing that you can improve." It blew my overthinking mind, especially as someone who worked in higher education, specifically on the scholarship of teaching and learning. It taught me much about mindsets and their power in shaping your future. I assumed that with the right mindset, I could focus on a goal and achieve it. Still, with me having a freaking fixed mindset regarding publishing in particular, the moment I failed specific tasks or objectives, it was hard not to give up completely, and sometimes I did.

Academia is a challenging world no matter what, but if you are "lucky" enough to work at an excellent university and have tenure, researching and publishing articles regularly, and often at least one whole book, is a standard job requirement. There's a saying in higher education at more prestigious institutions: "Publish or Perish." And I felt that pressure constantly. I did publish a fair amount, but it's also a known quantity in academia that many journals, especially the top ones, have meager acceptance rates. So, it should be no surprise that I submitted articles for publication and got rejection letters more than once. Many writers and scholars will resubmit their work if they get helpful feedback from the editors, but I only resubmitted a rejected article once. It was denied again. Yeah, that's right, it was rejected twice, and I didn't resubmit it to see if the third time would be the charm! In fact, I didn't bother reworking and resubmitting any subsequent rejections I received. I considered all those cases closed.

Academia can be an absolute confidence crusher for ADHDers like me who, for one, didn't know I had ADHD and suffered from debilitating imposter syndrome. Don't get me wrong. I faked it well enough to fool everyone, but that job stressed me out nonstop. Here's the thing: I am my harshest critic, especially when facing adversity, but once I began to reflect on my triumphs, I started to realize that although being a professor had been a demanding career for me, it had also been highly enriching and had taught me loads of transferable skills that could be so valuable outside of academia. Once I realized this, a bit of positive self-talk did wonders not only for my mood but for my mindset, too. If I could have kids, a job, a house, etc., I could find the time and motivation to chase my dreams. My real dreams.

Many businesses have cultivated a growth mindset among their employees to increase innovation, creativity, and motivation. You've likely heard of startups or small companies that only work for four days a week instead of five. This helps employees' well-being, which also improves productivity. A happy worker is a good worker, just like Wonka's Oompa Loompas (though working in a chocolate factory would make anyone happy). Some businesses cultivating a growth mindset are likely incredible to work for; they boast stellar benefits, provide opportunities for learning with workshops and training programs, offer coaching, and help employees set challenging goals that align with the company's mission and vision. According to the Harvard Business Review, employees who have a growth mindset are

- 47% likelier to say that their colleagues are trustworthy,
- 34% likelier to feel a strong sense of ownership and commitment to the company,
- 65% likelier to state that the company supports risk-taking and
- 49% likelier to say that the company fosters innovation (Fuller & Shikaloff, 2016).

They say you should always lead by example, and people with a growth mindset tend to encapsulate it greatly. I recall a story from my friend Pisli when she first started working in the hospitality industry. She worked as a receptionist in a fancy hotel and hated it. Pisli had so many fantastic ideas for the hotel, but her manager (whom we'll call Dick) often disregarded them, saying it would waste time and money. Whenever Pisli did something wrong, Dick would scold her without providing feedback. Pisli felt like she had to walk on eggshells constantly when he was around. Dick would often praise other employees over Pisli, whom she proclaimed were born with more talent than her or at least had a leg up because their native language was English (Pisli was from Spain and felt she was subject to a degree of discrimination because she was foreign and spoke with a thick accent). To put it simply, Dick was, well, a complete d - - - . Never mind. Pisli eventually left the job and found a position in another hotel where she felt appreciated for her skills, insights, ideas, *and* native Spanish language. Her new job allowed her to thrive, and many incentives resulted in her becoming a human resources manager with a growth mindset.

If you don't work in an environment/with people who cultivate a growth mindset, get out, GET OUT NOW! Alternatively, you can take these baby steps toward developing *your* growth mindset:

- **Overlook imperfection.** If you expect everything to be perfect, you've been watching too many Disney movies. Embrace imperfection. Own that shit! Perfectionism is creating a false reality in which everything must run smoothly (most of us don't live in Oz). It's either all or nothing with pesky perfectionism. Acknowledge that things aren't always going to appear perfect and that this is ok. If you always have high expectations, you can anticipate disappointment, right?

- **Unleash your inner badass.** Don't shy away from challenges. When challenges arise, you can see them as opportunities for growth. By shifting your perspective, you can see something new and different as an experience that will likely benefit you for the greater good. Only once we are out of our comfort zone do we truly grow. You're not the only person out of 7 billion in the world to get scared when faced with a serious challenge. You could even challenge yourself by doing things you never thought of, such as streaking during a football game. Do it during the Super Bowl halftime show, and maybe the record number of spectators worldwide will simply believe it's part of the act! Coach yourself on exploring new circumstances and experiences. It may sound cheesy, but think of how exciting and new the challenge is. Yes, I used cliché words like "exciting" and "new"... because they are utterly appropriate. Throw yourself into the deep end. The more you get accustomed to embracing challenges, the easier they become as you uncover abilities and skills you didn't even know you had. You're a badass. You know that, right?
- **Don't allow yourself to wield words like weapons** —negative words, I mean. Pay attention to the words you say or think because if they are low or dark, they can manifest into your psyche. Seriously. Censor yourself if need be. Not with cuss words. You can fucking fling those around all you want, and you should if it helps you. What I mean is, replace negative thoughts with positive ones to help build your growth mindset. And if you need to throw a cuss word in there to help motivate you,

fucking do it. I know, I know. It can be tricky, and I am not advocating for any toxic positivity bullshit. But we're not talking about specific feelings here due to the loss of a job or the death of a loved one. We are talking about the general way that you use language. Instead of thinking, "I can't cook this absurdly large pizza," replace it with, "I am going to cook the shit out of this enormous Italian pie, and it's going to be fucking magnificent!" Instead of judgment, focus on acceptance. Replace hate with compassion. Stop disrespecting yourself and hold yourself to higher thoughts; your decisions and consequences will reflect that. And you fucking deserve compassion, not just from others, but also and more importantly from yourself. OK, enough F-words here. I think you get my point.

- **Don't brown-nose.** You've likely seen a colleague trying to get approval from the boss, with their nose so far up their ass that they can taste chocolate, but it doesn't get them anywhere. If we want a growth mindset, the only approval we need to seek is our own. Learn to self-accept, trust yourself, and know the only one you need to impress is yourself. Nobody else. Anyways, kissing up is exhausting. The lesson? Treat yourself before treating someone else.

- **Find your inner punk.** Punk ethos is all about being authentic and giving zero fucks what others think of you. So, find your radically authentic self. Having a growth mindset means being genuine, not only about your goals and success but also about yourself. If you have always pretended to be someone else, then you are what many neurotypical high-school students would refer to as "fake." Cheers to us, late-diagnosed "I masked my whole life" ADHDers. I see you! And it's not too late to unmask! Developing your authentic self can take some time, but once you do, you will find more drive to pursue your goals and chase your wildest dreams. One tip is to dress more authentically, basically, however the fuck you want. If you always love to wear Crocs but only have one pair, go out and buy six so you can wear a pair every day of the week. Rock that shit. And just because you see yourself as a business person or entrepreneur doesn't mean you have to wear suits Monday through Thursday and polos and jeans for "Casual Friday." If you are comfortable in your own skin, you will feel whatever part you are meant to play. You make the rules.

- **Purpose produces progress.** Cultivating a sense of purpose can clarify what you want to set goals on in life. Take some time to define your purpose, whether it's giving back to the community, owning a business, or trying every flavor of ice cream at Baskin Robbins like my best friend, Tracy, and I did one summer back in high school. Anyone with a growth mindset typically has a sense of purpose, reinforcing every decision and action they take. List the top three things you always wanted (and it better not be live, laugh, love).

- **Know your strengths and weaknesses.** People with a growth mindset will appreciate their strengths while actively seeking ways to grow and learn. If you are great at telling stories but need help writing them, focus on how you could. Growth mindset folks enjoy learning because it is stimulating and essential to their personal and professional development as a human being. It's that simple. Knowledge is power. If you have never attended a conference on something you're interested in, a talk by an author or expert you admire, a workshop for a skill you want to acquire, or an online course you can complete in your own time, break the cycle, and do it. Why not?

- **Not all criticism will kill you.** Criticism aims to improve things, so don't take it personally when someone gives you invaluable suggestions or tips that will benefit you. If anything, we should all adopt a more open mind to constructive criticism and explore it. If you are open to hearing some harsh truths, it may help you in the long run. Ask yourself, "Instead of giving the middle finger, how can I use this feedback to help myself?" Believe me, working in academia made me an expert in taking criticism since administrators evaluated my job performance, and students rated my teaching and their learning every single semester. Sometimes that shit hurt, and occasionally, it was unwarranted; but overall, it was meant to help me grow and learn as a teacher, scholar, and mentor, and in general, it did. My 17 cents (adjusted for inflation)? In the end, take feedback with a grain of salt, or sugar if that suits you better, and consider it genuinely. More often than not, it's not personal.

- **Allow mistakes to motivate you.** Even better? Learn to laugh at your own if at all possible. With a fixed mindset, you are much less likely to take risks or make mistakes; however, learning from the mistakes of others can reduce the fear of trying something new. If a friend went skydiving and forgot their parachute, which is the only time you can, then if you decided to try it, you would surely remember to take your parachute (or, maybe, never ever try skydiving). Don't worry about making mistakes in front of other people, either; this happens at some point in all our lives; it's human nature. One of Janet Jackson's tits got exposed during the halftime show of the Super Bowl back in 2004, and she probably sold more albums because of it. I wish I could have seen into the future when I was 11, and my left boob fell out of my swimsuit as I crashed into the water at full speed off of a water slide at Water Country USA the summer before 7th grade. Maybe I would have been less horrified by it.

- **Slow down.** Thanks to so many things in this digital age, like streaming platforms and delivery services, when we want something, we want it NOW! So, is it possible that when trying to reach the end result of a task or goal, we want to get there faster? Absolutely. Who doesn't? But here's the thing: with a growth mindset, focusing on the process instead of the end product usually improves results. For example, if you want to become a black belt in karate, there are a bunch of other belts to get first. You can't simply become a black belt by winning a fight with someone who is a black belt. There's a joke in here somewhere, but let's stay on task for once.

- **Act with a punk attitude.** Remember when our parents told us as kids that having an attitude was a bad thing? They were all, "HEY, watch your attitude!" They didn't mention it was the opposite when we became adults. Attitude is not when you misbehave and stick out your tongue in protest; it's a combination of thoughts, beliefs, and, most importantly, behaviors that shape your thinking. Attitude is punk, and it's about being true to yourself without being unkind to others. To remold your fixed mindset into a growing one, you need to make an effort and take the time to establish it. Again, channel your inner punk. I know it's in there.

The beauty of a growth mindset is that as it develops and you see results from hitting goals, it springboards you into new areas of interest you never contemplated before. If you desire to become a singer and do everything to become one, you may realize you intend to learn an instrument next. It's like a domino effect in that way, when you are no longer afraid to try new things and discover, grow, and flourish.

Remember that cultivating a growth mindset is not about the end result but the journey of getting there. Ugh, that word "journey" again, but you know what I mean. The process might feel long and arduous and could feel as long as a *Lord of the Rings* movie, but I know just how to make it so much easier. Get your ass to the next chapter to find out what the hell I am talking about.

———

Key takeaway: Unleash your inner punk so you can cultivate the shit out of a growth mindset!

CHAPTER SEVEN

MINDFUL MOCKERY?
HELL YES!

"MY OVERTHINKING IS SO creative and advanced, it could write a bestselling novel – too bad it's a tragicomedy about my life." – Sara Toninstan (getting used to it yet?)

As I worked to sharpen my growth mindset, I was getting myself out there. More recently, I attended conferences on start-ups, workshops on social media marketing, and did online courses on anything that interested me. I had a yearning to learn. The thing was, though, that it was tough, too. I was trying to shift from a fixed mindset of being stuck in the same job until I died, which came with all the lovely negativity, to the growth mindset whose benefits seemed so hard to reach. I had doubts and fears about being my own boss and running my own business one day. I was unsure about myself and the path I was trying to take. When you spend so much of your life not believing in yourself, it's hard to become the opposite, harder than doing a marathon on crutches. Nevertheless, I still managed to coach myself to get out more and experience more than usual. It's why and how this book probably exists and thus how you're reading it right now!

SO, I was attending a stand-up comedy night, and the main headliner surprised the shit out of me. It wasn't offensive humor or terrible jokes, but an older woman. This woman must have been in her 70s. She came up on the stage and started telling jokes about how great it is that everyone gives her a seat and how the last time she had sex, you couldn't buy sliced bread. The lady even made jokes about how she hoped this wouldn't be her final gig. The whole room was in hysterics with laughter. It was nothing anybody expected. As she finished her set, she received a standing ovation. I loved it! I couldn't stop thinking about it. How can this woman at her ripe age be so ballsy and not give a flying shit? She COMPLETELY subverted expectations and delivered on the humor. I needed a good laugh that night, but I didn't expect it to have me laughing so hard it hurt. I couldn't even remember the last time I had done that. If anything, the experience was refreshing and inspirational and gave me a much-needed push about my own life.

There are many styles of humor, from deadpan to dark to slapstick. Still, this badass self-proclaimed "old spinster" was using self-deprecating humor. Simply put, she made fun of herself. We are all guilty of doing it, but as overthinkers with anxiety, nobody is around to hear the punchline. So many comedians do this brand of humor and with good reason. I think it's a lot healthier than making fun of others (though some bitches out there deserve it). One of the big no-nos to overcoming anxiety and developing a growth mindset is a surplus of negative thoughts; however, what if you could use any remotely negative thoughts you had to your advantage? Humor is always good. Have you ever met a funny person you never liked? Learning to make fun of ourselves helps us reach that incredible growth mindset in some compelling ways, such as:

- **Gaining perspective and humility:** The power of self-deprecating humor allows us to step back and recognize and acknowledge our perceived flaws and imperfections. By joking and making fun of our imperfections, like how you may always arrive late or refuse to eat spicy food because of a temperamental anus, we develop a sense of humility and acknowledge that nobody is perfect. We don't need to be either.
- **Breaking the cycle of perfectionism:** Perfectionism causes us anxiety and creates an overwhelming fear of failure. However, self-deprecating humor can serve as a tool to break free from that vicious cycle of trying to make everything "right." If you can see opportunities to make fun of your mistakes, you can see that making mistakes is also part of life.
- **Building resilience:** If you can learn to laugh at yourself and not take yourself too seriously, then you build the resilience to bounce back from challenges and failures, too. Self-deprecating humor helps us approach difficult situations with more ease and focus positively. The more you laugh at failures or mistakes, the better equipped you are to deal with the next one.

There has always been this false belief that some people are just funny and others are not (thanks, fixed mindset!). Anyone can become funny and learn to observe life's trials and tribulations and make jokes about it. At times, we often find ourselves being self-deprecating without really knowing it. In the past, anytime someone tried to compliment me, maybe about my shoes, I would joke that they were my mom's or overshare and blurt out exactly where I got them and what major sale they were on (thanks, ADHD!). If my students told me that class that day had been super engaging, I would brush it off and tell them how much more I had hoped we could cover. Sometimes, we self-deprecate because we want to avoid seeming arrogant or smug. We downplay ourselves in a way to appear more humble, and we hesitate to give off a big ego vibe. If you won the lottery today, you might tell everyone how you don't deserve it (or produce a video of you with a monocle and a cigar dangling from your mouth, laughing hysterically on a bed of cold hard cash).

Unfortunately, there's usually also a con for every pro in life. It's essential to know the risks of self-deprecation, such as how doing it too often can affect your self-esteem. Then again, if you suffer from anxiety and overthinking, everything affects your self-esteem (or at least can feel like it). I know when my anxiety seemed to be raging hard, the simplest thing could make me lose confidence, like changing my profile picture on Facebook to something obtuse that I thought was funny but no one got it. If everything will affect you and affect your esteem and anxiety, why not at least try utilizing self-deprecating humor to counteract it and see if it changes things?

We discussed before how negative thinking leads to negative reality, and sometimes, making self-deprecating jokes can fall flat. If you hear crickets based on self-critical remarks about yourself, maybe learn to never use that joke again or try one that's not shit. It could also be an indicator that you took it too far. When you are too harsh on yourself, people notice, and it's a vibe killer, for sure. Silence can tell you a lot about how self-deprecating you are, but is that a reason to stop trying? There's still no reason to ignore its perks. With anything in life, it's all about finding the balance (Hakuna Mattata! Or whatever).

Making a joke at your own expense can be seen as a coping mechanism, with studies implying that it is more positive than negative (Owens, 1993; Speer, 2019). Remember my friend Johnny from Chapter 1 and his bagpipe butt comment? Yeah, well, it turns out there's evidence-based research out there that backs up his making his bagpipe butt the butt of his own joke. (Are you still with me?!) A study by researchers at the University of Granada challenges previous assumptions and beliefs regarding self-deprecating humor. Contrary to common belief, the study revealed that self-deprecating humor is not always associated with adverse effects. In fact, it was found to be connected to greater emotional well-being, indicating higher scores in psychological and emotional well-being, including happiness (Torres-Marín, Navarro-Carrillo, & Carretero-Dios, 2017).

Laughing gives us an immediate boost of dopamine, making us feel so damn good. Making others laugh with jokes based on yourself gives them dopamine, too; it's like being a dopamine drug dealer. Mocking ourselves is sometimes a great deflector when faced with social situations. However, it's sometimes the better way to deal with sticky situations. If you were playing poker and kept losing, you might feel better about losing by commenting on how much you suck. What matters is if you have a high enough sense of self-worth. With a growth mindset, your sense of self-worth SHOULD come hand-in-hand with how you align your goals and success. So maybe poking fun at your own expense isn't so bad? I digress; using more self-deprecating humor was the best thing I found during my personal quest towards developing a growth mindset. And to be honest, even in the more fixed mindset of my youth, I still slung self-deprecating humor around like it was trending on TikTok. Not everything will go as planned, and not everything will be perfect, but in those moments, you can surely laugh about it, right?

We learned how valuable comedy is and the benefits that come with it, so you might be wondering how self-deprecating humor is any different? The times have changed so drastically regarding humor. Picture this, you are meeting married friends for a luncheon and a game of bridge in 1963. They lightly joke about their mundane married life and partners, and from out of nowhere, you make a self-deprecating joke about faking an orgasm during sex. Your married friends would literally clutch their pearls in shock, and that was the last time you would ever go to a luncheon with friends. Now, we have memes, TikTok and YouTube, publications like *The Onion* and *The Hard Times*, and so many sources of self-deprecating humor (and it's made our lives so much more fun). One way we can positively disrupt our lives is by becoming more self-deprecating. Allow me to suggest some of the perks of undertaking this genre of humor over all the rest:

- **It's so attainable.** In the fixed mindset, it's assumed that some people are funny and some are not. This couldn't be further from the goddamn truth. We all have something about ourselves to laugh about, whether it's a quality, characteristic, circumstance, or bad habit. We are our own best source of material.
- **It's self-expressive.** What better way to showcase your dynamic, and maybe occasionally wacky, personality than with self-deprecating humor. When you aren't afraid to poke fun at yourself, you ooze confidence and highlight how comfortable you are in your skin by making light of challenging scenarios or situations.

- **It builds social connections.** There are so many great ice-breakers out there, such as "Would you rather have two truths or one lie," however, self-deprecating humor trumps them all. When you laugh at yourself, others are drawn to you. Showing how at ease you are as yourself also indicates you are less judgmental of others' flaws. It makes you relatable and likable and helps build strong relationships. As mentioned, making fun of yourself can also help you in many awkward situations. If you accidentally got locked in your bathroom and were finally found after three days, and it was all over the news, you could save yourself a lot of embarrassment by making self-deprecating jokes about it. You could say, "I knew my life was going to shit, but I had no clue how far down the toilet it was actually heading!" Research shows that people think it's an attractive trait in a long-term partner to make jokes, and it may even enhance their attractiveness. (Grammer, 1990) Just be sure you don't downplay your skills or undermine yourself so much that people fake laugh to feel sorry for you.
- **It boosts self-esteem.** I know I am repeating myself (but how else can you learn?) Mistakes are a big part of our lives, and instead of cringing over failures about the past or present, we can choose to reflect and laugh. Self-deprecating humor is perfect for maintaining a funny outlook in challenging scenarios and benefits self-esteem and well-being.
- **It diffuses tension.** I am sure you experienced a moment when things were tense, and you made a joke to break it. It's like when two friends are having a drunken argument about the silliest shit,

and you intervene with a relatable self-deprecating remark about yourself. If you were stuck in a meeting at work and things were getting heated over who forgot to turn off the office coffee maker or some other bullshit, you could interject and say, "At least no one forgot to turn off the air-conditioner last night so you didn't all have to sit here and stare at my hard nipples this morning!" Well, maybe don't use that one, but you know what I mean. Pro tip: Know your audience!

- **It's a coping mechanism.** In this day and age, we can all agree we need some kind of coping mechanism. Turning on the news only subjects us to negativity, likely about how everything is killing us and we are all killing each other. You probably can't even drink water anymore. The news is miserable and constant, too. Making fun of ourselves, especially when we get overwhelmed after reading or watching all the gloom and doom, will make us feel better. Having a chuckle at yourself can keep those shitty thoughts at bay. It can lift you up when you are down.

- **It's empowering.** Making witty, sarcastic, or dare I say, crass remarks about yourself shows vulnerability, which breaks down barriers with others and encourages them to do the same. Why hide from our mistakes when we can flaunt our flaws instead? There is nothing more empowering than owning your shit and taking pride in it.

- **It can lead to Eustress.** Wait, what? What the fuck is Eustress? Eustress is a paradox: it's positive stress, people! There is a thing called positive stress? Yep. Who knew? Well, now YOU do. Eustress is a beneficial type of stress that helps with motivation, performance, and well-being. Negative stress can get detrimental and overwhelming, but with Eustress, you feel a sense of excitement and personal growth. By harnessing humor, we can positively deal with stress. I did many so many presentations, taught so many classes, and led so many meetings as a professor and constantly used self-deprecating humor to make it all more fun. I guarantee you, none of my former students or colleagues will ever remember me as boring.

So, how do we become more self-deprecating? Is there some course or workshop worth attending? Do we need to sleep with a comedian?

Don't sleep with a comedian; there is not enough improv. You're better off sleeping with a clown. Scratch that; you don't need to sleep with anyone. One of the simplest ways to self-deprecate is through the medium of affirmations. An affirmation is a positive statement or declaration, one often used to help reinforce an attitude or desired belief. When used, it's a powerful weapon, as it can help motivate your mindset and dispel self-limiting beliefs. Every main character in a Disney movie uses a positive affirmation before some big event. Affirmations can be positive and can also become beneficial with a sprinkle of self-deprecation.

Next time you are stressing out or facing a challenge or experiencing something awkward, try giving your negative thoughts a self-deprecating affirmative spin. If you get in the habit of doing this enough, you can train your brain to spin almost anything adverse in a more positive light, and that, my friends is a gift. Here are some slightly "lame but you get the picture" examples:

- This situation is awkward but could be worse; I could be naked, too!
- I might be late, but I'm stylish. Yeah, the expression *fashionably late*? That's based on me.
- This challenge is nothing compared to forcing myself out of bed.
- This situation seems dire, but at least I still have teeth.
- I need to push myself, which I've done many times before when constipated.
- My anxiety is so bad I can be worried about everything and nothing all at once! Impressive, right?
- My anxiety is so bad that I spend all my time worrying about things that haven't even happened yet. But hey, at least I'm prepared!
- I'm so anxious that it's become my daily reminder that I'm still alive. I mean, something has to keep me going, right?
- They say losers worry—well, I guess that makes me a champion!
- Anxiety? That's just my way of telling myself, "You can do better!"
- I'm so clumsy that I trip over nothing...but hey, at least I'm always entertaining!
- My memory is so bad that I forget what I was going to worry about--thank you, _____ (insert anything appropriate here: ADHD, menopause, repressed childhood trauma, too much weed in college, etc.).
- My sense of direction is so bad that it's become a running joke—if I say turn left, you'd better turn right!

- I'm so indecisive that I can't even decide which worry to worry about first—guess that solves the problem of having too many options.
- My brain is wired in such a way that it's always thinking of new ways to worry—yay, ADHD!

Affirmations for the wary or downright cynical seem not worth trying, but if you never try, you'll never know. If you do try, though, you'll know, you know? Sorry, I couldn't resist. If the above affirmations aren't your thing and seem too generalized, make your own. There is something so rewarding about coming up with your own joke. Conjuring up a bunch of funny affirmations can empower you like never before.

Here's how to make your own healthy, self-deprecating affirmations and not when you are having a total meltdown:

- **Step one:** Choose a topic you would enjoy making fun of about yourself (though be somewhat nice too). It could be anything from your lateness to clumsiness to lousy luck to the inability to find two matching pairs of socks.
- **Step two:** Brainstorm ideas on ways to make fun of the topic in a light-hearted and funny way.
- **Step three:** Put those ideas and concepts on paper (or Google doc) and refine them until they feel right.
- **Step four:** Once you get the affirmations down, practice them by speaking them out loud with a smile, which helps reinforce them.
- **Step five:** Now you have the affirmations down, arm yourself with them whenever you need them most. Whenever you feel anxious or nervous or

about to face some daunting challenge, use them, and use them well.

Self-deprecating humor is a powerful tool when used effectively. It can help dissolve sticky situations, break down barriers, and offer us a much-needed fresh perspective in the present. It's also important to note that self-worth and self-compassion should always be a priority, too, if not THE priority over anything. When faced with tough choices or challenges, laughing at yourself can unleash tension and make the situation bearable. The strong and successful tend to make fun of themselves and their situations, which helps them cope and strive to progress.

Self-deprecating humor is not for everyone; it might not even work for everyone. That said, I am not giving up on you, even when you try to do it yourself. At times when I didn't feel like cracking a joke, I did something else, I got moving. Walking, running, jumping, climbing, swimming, anything that involves using my body, and even if you think it's something you can't do, the next chapter will convince you otherwise.

———

Key takeaway: Self-deprecating humor can help you alleviate your anxiety.

CHAPTER EIGHT

LET'S GET PHYSICAL: REWARD YOUR BODY INSTEAD OF PUNISHING IT

"THE FIRST TIME I see a jogger smiling, I'll consider it!"
— Joan Rivers

Everywhere we turn, we see an image of a mid-level, universally good-looking influencer promoting a brand or lifestyle. A lot of them have a tan and are on a beach holding some jar of energy drink that tastes like crap (though crap might taste better). Whether on a billboard, on Instagram and TikTok, on YouTube, or even on an abandoned halfway house poster, the luxury of looking good has never been more visual. Sex sells; ask any successful prostitute, but it's nothing new. When I was growing up in the 80's, fitness fanatics were everywhere, too. So many bodybuilder action heroes dominated the big screen. Even Jane Fonda built a fitness empire by selling cardio workout videos where she jumped around for 30 minutes in a French-cut silky spandex leotard and leg warmers. And I was there for it.

Yep. I totally bought into it. Workout videos were getting rented more in video stores than porno flicks. Not that I would know anything about that. It seemed as though the fad to lose fat and "get sexy" was taking over the world. The thing is, when we are over-exposed to all this poser propaganda, we become acclimatized to it. It doesn't make you want to go and work out. Worse, if you have anxiety or over-think, it makes you compare yourself and think that you could never look that "good." The truth is, you don't need to look good. Looking good is subjective; you need to *feel* good. Physical exercise, for many, is about how it makes them look, but c'mon, the best perks of exercise – and something greatly overlooked – are how it makes you feel mentally.

As overthinkers, we give our minds a workout five, six, or ten times a minute, but it's getting physical that will freaking benefit us. Approximately 50% of the global population will be diagnosed with a mental health disorder at some point in their lives (McGrath et al., 2023). Read that again: roughly HALF of all inhabitants on Planet Earth can expect to develop a mental health disorder that usually emerges in childhood, adolescence, or young adulthood, and that can discourage anyone, but especially young folks, from seeking health-promoting activities (Larion, 2014).

You'd think getting in shape with fitness apps, watches, and online coaches would be easier. It definitely seems like we associate technology with comfort now; I mean, isn't it designed to simplify our lives? When I open an app on my iPhone 14 Pro, it's typically because I need downtime. I need to chill and rejuvenate through the magic of 21st century distractions. The big issue for me is that my brain goes on vacation the moment I open Instagram, and my fingers take over faster than the speed of gossip. They start scrolling and clicking on everything except the relaxing content I wanted. The next thing I know, I'm over on YouTube, 37 videos deep into a conspiracy theory about how pigeons are actually government spies (I always thought it was crows …).

And this is where my anxiety and overthinking kick in.

Instead of laughing it off, I start to wonder if there's any truth to it. Suddenly, I'm suspicious of every feathered rat I see on the street. Am I being watched? Recorded? Before I know it, I've spent hours devising a plan to outsmart these ridiculous "secret agents" (even though I have nothing to hide!), completely forgetting about my initial quest for relaxation. So much for using the Internet to escape my overthinking – now I'm just paranoid about pigeons!

I've always been in pretty decent shape. So, what finally kickstarted me hardcore into fitness? It sure as hell wasn't a sensational Jane Fonda workout video on VHS or a scary dream of Rambo bursting into my bedroom as I slept holding a celery stick instead of a combat knife. I just ran. Yep, it sounds so simple, but it worked. I didn't even plan to. I was 21, working through college with three jobs and taking six classes my last year. On one particularly stressful day, ready to implode, as I slowly paced to my car to go home from the pizza shop where I was a delivery driver, I had this sudden urge to just fucking sprint. Maybe I felt like when I got home, I could finally relax, but before I did, I wanted to do a serious drain of my hyperactive brain. Going for a run seemed like a better alternative to relieve stress than screaming in the middle of the strip mall parking lot. Luckily, there was a trail in the adjacent woods to run into, which was way better than running into oncoming traffic. It was chaotic because it was dark; I was maneuvering around people, jumping over dog turds, and ducking under tree branches. But, the stress, negative thoughts, and overthinking were no longer present. My mind was on constant alert as I ran, giving me that much-needed distraction that things like arcade games back then or social media today ultimately couldn't. I was literally running from my problems, but at least I felt better afterward. At that moment, I was free, like a tiger that escaped the zoo.

Later on, in my thirties right after my kids were born and

pregnancy, child birth, and nursing had wreaked havoc on my entire body, I opted to try a gym, and I was offered a free session with a personal trainer, under the lure of paying for future sessions. Fair enough! I told him I wanted to tone up, and he referred to nutrition (something we rarely used to hear about in America). If I buy these future sessions, I asked him, will I be able to drink beer and still get toned up? He told me no. And that, my AFAB, AMAB, and trans ladies & gentlemen, demigirls & boys, my bi, pan & agender babes, drag queens, and non-binary anti-royalists was the first and last time I tried personal training. I wanted a 6-pack, sure, but at the time, I wanted the beer more than the abs. I tried yoga, and I wanted so badly to love it; but yoga requires introspection and forces you to sit with yourself by yourself, and I simply wasn't at a point in my life where I was ready to that. It was all too quiet. The overthinking and negative thoughts can still flood in. Running was what worked for me for a long time, and it's competitive as shit, too, even if the only person I was willing to compete with was myself. If I could run a mile in under nine minutes, I could try to hit two in under seventeen minutes, then try for three under twenty-five minutes.

Running was, for me, the catalyst for short-term mental relief and long-term relief over time. If I hadn't tried it, I would have never known. Not only was it a distraction, but as I got into running, jogging, or any form of physical movement, I felt more in control of my thoughts. Your body rewards you for taking care of it, my fellow overthinkers, except when you eat spicy food. My point is that sometimes, the best approach when you are feeling overwhelmed with anxiety is to take immediate action, physical action. The intensity of that first real run at 21 gave me immediate gratification; however, with consistency, it would yield compound effects over time. It gave me superpowers. Okay, maybe it did not. But I felt pretty damn good, and at some point, I did get close to getting the 6-pack of abs I had previously shunned in favor of ice-cold IPAs. I was having less and less anxiety-induced moments, and when I was stressed, it never lasted nearly as long as before I got all physical. What my undiagnosed ADHD younger self did not know is that intense cardiovascular exercise is really effective at staving off that ADHD-induced anxiety. In retrospect, it makes complete sense that running made me high. More than my body, my brain grew to crave it, unbeknownst to me.

Exercise is highly regarded for helping improve us physically, but the mental perks are just as good, if not for anyone with anxiety or issues with overthinking, even better. Feeling skeptical? I was until I did one of my famous rabbit-hole deep dives online (which took way longer back in the dark ages of ye-olde dial-up Internet). I soon discovered that the mental benefits of exercise included the following:

- **Quells depression and anxiety:** Science has proven that exercise is a mood booster, helping alleviate symptoms of anxiety and depression. When doing anything physical, the body releases endorphins as a delightful reward, making you feel happier and sometimes euphoric. And here I had thought weed was the only savior. My bad!
- **Minimizes stress:** It's no secret that stress is a total bastard, but with some exercise, you can reduce stress. By increasing our heart rate, we can reverse stress-induced brain damage through the stimulation of neurohormones such as norepinephrine, which significantly improves our cognition, mood, but also thinking in general (especially when shit thoughts cloud our minds). Through exercise, we also force the central and sympathetic nervous systems of our body to

communicate better with each other, resulting in an improvement in how our body handles stress.

- **Boosts self-esteem and self-confidence:** You feel proud when you reach a fitness goal, whether it's to lose weight, gain muscle, or beat a personal best record from running around. You feel like all your hard work has led you to achieve so much. You find as you improve physically that your mental health improves as well.

- **Promotes better sleep:** A good night's sleep is hard to come by when you are an overthinker, but with exercise, things can shift in your favor. When getting physical activity, we increase body temperature, resulting in a calming effect in our brains. Exercise will also improve the body's built-in alarm clock, AKA the circadian rhythm. It's responsible for controlling when we feel alert or tired.

- **Boosts brain function:** Exercise gives our stupid, overthinking brains a considerable boost. It helps strengthen memory by creating new brain cells, a process known as neurogenesis, which in turn helps to improve our brain's overall function and performance. It also stunts memory loss and cognitive decline by strengthening the hippocampus, the part of our brain responsible for learning and memory. Physical activity also boosts creativity, so running, jogging, or walking around like a crab literally has the ability to inspire you.

Running is a big step, well, many, many fast steps, actually, and I get that it's not for everyone. You get all sweaty, and you might slip on a banana peel and accidentally perform a back handspring twisting somersault cartwheel and thus inadvertently join a circus. I'm very pro-clown and have always been a clown, but my life is already enough of a circus without actually having to join one. Heck, if you are running and not paying attention, you could run into a hornet's nest or, worse, your ex. As I have gotten older and more in control of my anxiety and overthinking, running outside (and admittedly even on treadmills to what some-times felt like oblivion) has helped me enormously. I can honestly say that there were also times when running pretty much saved my life.

But in recent years, I even started overthinking my progress with running and pushed myself so hard one day that I injured myself. I hobbled to the doctor and then a massage therapist, hoping they knew witchcraft. They both told me to take a break from running but still try to move as much as possible. So yeah, I had to stop for a while, and although it was pretty hard for me to do cold turkey, I decided to do something even more radically mindful than running:

I took a walk.

Well, it was more like shuffling at first, but eventually, my hamstring injury healed enough to start moving again, and that's when I uncovered the beauty of walking. With walking, I never got too sweaty; I could more easily avoid bumping into someone I disliked by simply doing a U-turn. I wasn't worried about tripping over tree roots or stumbling on a rock on the sidewalk, which would lead to my ankle giving way, which would, in turn, make me fall off the sidewalk and then into the road, where a car would inevitably plow me down. Nope. At times, when I am stressed, close to pulling my hair out or deleting my Facebook for the 6th time in a month, I tell myself: "Self, just go for a damn walk."

Moving in some form or another is still better than staring out of a window and watching a neighbor struggle with parallel parking. A simple 20-minute walk, or even a 5-minute stroll, is still better than no walk at all. It's like when you were a kid, and you were being a little shit; the teacher might make you go for a short walk to the principal's office to clear your mind. As adults, going for a walk seems easy enough, except if you overthink and those negative, bothersome thoughts still sit with you. Then again, walking is much simpler than running and less chaotic, and if you pay attention to what you see, smell, and hear during a brisk stroll, you find that your mind is not nearly as clouded.

I remember seeing hardcore runners or even casual joggers dressed head to toe in nylon, expressionless faces; it didn't do much to persuade me to join them. With walking, you don't need to get dressed up; it's a walk, not a catwalk. I would go for a walk or a run in whatever I felt comfortable in (though don't try running in flip-flops). If you can get in 10,000 steps daily, that's five miles. It's a considerable number, and you don't even need to hit that many. You can start way lower and work towards setting personal goals. It's unfair of me to brag about my successful experiences with getting fit without acknowledging that some of you are perhaps utterly disinterested in it. That's ok, there are still other ways to get *physical*. Let's break this shit down.

- **Maniacal laughter:** The Joker, Batman's biggest nemesis, always laughed maniacally, and yet, could this be his secret to looking so slim? We mentioned the perks of laughter yoga in Chapter 1, and maniacal laughter is no different, if not a little more chaotic. There had been many times when I would force myself to fake laugh, but strangely, after one minute, I would start laughing for real, and I would laugh so hard sometimes that my stomach ached. These "fake" laughing sessions constituted more or less an abs workout, only more enjoyable. Fake laughing or cackling like a maniac is not only one of the best forms of laughing with and at yourself, but it's perfect for physical activity, too. I have come to realize that the advice "fake it 'til you make it" (well-intentioned though it may be) is actually not always good advice and rather can encourage folks like me with ADHD or other invisible disabilities to mask even more, which isn't healthy. But in this case, when fake laughter leads to real laughter, that can only be a good thing.

- **Hula hooping:** Who says kids get to have all the fun? Hula hooping is a fun physical activity that will put you in a good mood quickly and help you burn a few calories simultaneously. Try doing it with your waist, then move to your legs and then neck and your ass if it's big enough. Create a dance routine to show off and instantly impress and entertain your friends. You can even hula hoop while performing house chores; who knew doing the dishes could be so exhilarating?

- **Dance-offs:** Speaking of dance routines, getting into a dance-off with a friend, relative, or stranger can help shift your mood and get you moving. It's not uncommon to learn some funky moves from one of your parents or friends, and with the power of TikTok challenges, you can find an excuse to get more involved or, better yet, get into a dance-off. We as adults can take ourselves way too seriously. I get it. We are so busy and stressed, and our lives are complex. But listen to the rhythm and let your body do the talking instead of your overthinking mind. Put a pause on cynicism and try. You never know; you might uncover a new career.

- **Zorbing:** I remember a friend who had a pet hamster, and she would stick him into a ball to run around in. I don't speak hamster, but from how he ran all over the place, he was having the time of his life. With zorbing, we can be just like that hamster. You get inside a giant inflatable ball and run around. It's even more fun on water! My daughter did this for her birthday with friends one year, and it was hysterical.

- **Pole fitness:** Okay, so you don't need to have the life ambition of being a pole dancer for this. I'd be lying if I said I hadn't secretly fantasized about being a stripper … and I got to practice some moves more than once back in the day. Not in a strip club though. My roommates and I had a pole in our basement apartment my sophomore year of college, and we spent many an evening blasting music, holding on with one hand, leaning out, and swirling around until we were dizzy and dying laughing. Also, my partner and I stayed in an AirBnb in Brooklyn years ago on a trip to NYC, and guess what? Our AirBnb host was a stripper, and a sweet slippery pole graced the dead center of the apartment. Did we swing around it? You better fucking believe we did, and we have photos to prove it! Point being, practicing pole fitness can be fun and entertaining to you (and anyone who watches), but it also helps improve flexibility, gives your body a complete workout, and builds confidence. If you don't have a pole, you can find loads outside with a bit of creativity (such as traffic lights or street lights and playgrounds).

- **Martial arts:** *The Karate Kid* was such a great movie. You might disagree, but it was remade in the 2000s, so younger generations clearly find this story compelling as well. This tale of a teenage boy learning about discipline and perseverance to overcome his personal limiting beliefs and kick his bully's ass resonated with Gen Xers. The Internet didn't exist for me to look this up back in 1984, but I bet if you surveyed kids and parents back then, registration for martial arts classes probably increased exponentially after that film's release. A sequel series to the original films called *Cobra Kai* came out a few years ago, and renewed interest in the films from the 1980s soared as many of the original actors reprised their roles 35+ years later. We could research the Internet to detect a possible surge in martial arts class sign-ups after *Cobra Kai*'s initial release, but I have better things to do. Tell you what, though: it wouldn't surprise me! Signing up for a class in judo, kung fu, or even sumo gets you out into the world, helps you make friends, and keeps you fit, too. Also, if you ever get into trouble, you can protect yourself. (Okay, fine, I admit that I almost said "you could kick someone's ass," but this is an inclusive and safe space, and we should not promote violence.)
- **Trampolining:** If you have access to a trampoline, you can give yourself a high-energy workout that will help you *literally* reach new heights. Play fun music to bounce up and down like a GenXer in 1978 on a pogo stick… Note to self: add pogo sticking to this chapter if I ever put out a second

edition… Okay, where was I? Oh yes, trampolines. If you have no space for a trampoline, you can sometimes find classes to attend instead. It seems silly, but it's loads of fun and a great way to get physical. It's not hard to find trampolines online these days for very reasonable prices, so if jumping for joy is your thing, I highly recommend (from personal experience) the investment. Treat yourself for your birthday or the holidays, but be sure to get a safety net enclosure!

- **Hiking:** This is a bit like walking but on steroids. The beauty of hiking is that it's pretty much an adventure. With all the rocky terrain and unchartered paths, too, you develop better balance and coordination. A typical hike can last a few hours, but it's perfect for getting fresh air and giving you endurance. Start small, however, if you have never hiked before; otherwise, this physical activity is not worth exploring and can be treacherous and dangerous. It's harder than it looks. I don't mean to scare anyone away, but seriously, safety first! One of the best features of a good hike is reaching the top of a summit. It gives you a moment to enjoy a spectacular view and appreciate the achievement of actually reaching it.

Exercise can seem daunting if you have yet to try it consistently. But consistency is key. With an open mind, you can find a physical activity that suits *you*. In the pursuit of freeing yourself from your negative thoughts and anxiety, it's imperative not to take yourself so seriously. We must try making jokes at our own expense, poking fun at the things we exaggerate through overthinking, and finding that the life we want is on the other side of fear.

Our overthinking discourages us from trying anything new. It convinces us we are not capable of so many things and that staying in our comfort zone is less risky than leaving it. With no risk comes no reward. We see fit people all the time. We might not even contemplate getting in shape. The beauty is that you don't need to be *that* fit person; you just need to move your ass and reap the mental health benefits in doing so.

If getting off your ass is hard, let me suggest one thing: pursue a new passion, or rediscover an old one that used to bring you joy. Passion plays such an essential role in taking that first step in anything. The first time you might have wanted to learn guitar was because of seeing your favorite hair metal band live, or you decided to learn to drive because you love drag races. That same passion can work in finding something physical to do. We should ignore all those fitness fanatics who are able to see their own butthole and do it for ourselves and, more importantly, our mental health.

Getting physical has its perks for mental health, but every once in a while, we sometimes need to unleash whatever's been bugging us with a good old-fashioned rant. Sometimes, we can try anything and everything, but we need support. As much as adulting has taught us that we need to figure out so much on our own, it's rational to acknowledge that it's not the solution for everything. The next chapter examines the importance of seeking support when needed.

———

Key takeaway: Physical activities help us manage anxiety and overthinking. Now, move your ass!

CHAPTER NINE

IT TAKES A VILLAGE TO RAISE AN OVERTHINKER

"SOMETIMES IT'S NOT about finding a solution but finding someone who understands your problem."
— Unknown

Sometimes, I wish I could go onto a stage in front of a million people and tell everyone how I overcame my anxieties and overthinking with a magical pill or through a 7-day training course like it was a colonic detox. I often used a combination of tricks and techniques to help put my worrisome, overactive brain to bed. And a lot of the time, it worked. The problem is that with all life's ups and downs, you can end up with something so overwhelming that maybe all the things that used to work refuse to help you now. You are not a quitter if you have made it this far in the book. If anything, you refuse to quit and have spunk (the American expression, not the British one... look it up) because of it. So what happens when life gives us lemons and we can't make lemonade? We seek someone who knows the recipe. No one was more surprised than I was to discover a huge untapped support system in place for me on Instagram. If I hadn't started an account that I knew I wanted to dedicate to mental health humor, I probably would have never come across all the ADHD content there, realized that I have had ADHD my whole life, and subsequently sought a diagnosis. That support system changed my life. That said, I have no contact with most of those folks in the physical world, and social media isn't a replacement for close friends and family whom you get to see in real life, nor a qualified therapist or medical professional should you need one.

Not everyone will know the recipe to life lemons, lemon life, or life-flavored lemonade. The people who might understand the recipe you are looking for are people who know you and, more importantly, support you. A support system, a group of friends or family, can help us reach our goals when dealing with a particular crisis or lend an ear when we need to rant harder than a teacher on their summer "vacation." Sometimes, the people closest to us, who know us inside out and up and down, can offer the much-needed emotional support we desperately need.

Think for a moment when you were experiencing something so out of your depth that you felt nothing could take your mind off the issue or distract you. Did you turn to somebody for help? A wise grandparent? A rational best friend? A wise-cracking neighbor who is always the glass half-full? A random stranger willing to hear you out? No matter the person or people, their presence is invaluable. You are not an island surrounded by the ocean and nothing else. It's good to reach out to your support system, cathartic even. It can seem challenging to look for guidance based on past experiences or insecurities, which is a sign of strength and not weakness, just so you know. If anything, a range of benefits to having a support system in place includes:

- **A sense of belonging:** Maybe we can't choose our family because I understand not everyone is close to theirs, but we can pick our friends and treat them equally. Whether it's family or friends, they can help us thrive and flourish through their support. A sense of belonging gives us security and acceptance, making us feel comfortable enough to open up much more quickly. Notably, a support system of people genuinely caring for your well-being will help alleviate loneliness or isolation during challenging times.

- **Emotional support:** A support system presents a safe, non-judgmental space to express our feelings, have a massive rant, or discuss our challenges. The emotional support loved ones offer can help us cope with stress, anxiety, or challenging situations that life can sometimes hand us.

- **Improved resilience and reduced stress:** A robust support system helps us to navigate better through uncertain territory. We can drastically reduce our stress levels when support comes from guidance, advice, or a fresh perspective. The proper support can also help us find challenges more manageable, and with reinforced encouragement and motivation, we can bounce back faster.

- **Improved self-confidence:** Having people believe in you when you don't believe in yourself can boost your self-esteem and confidence to help you deal with challenges or situations. Positive feedback can amplify our self-worth, empowering us to go above and beyond or tackle challenges head-on with renewed confidence.

A support system is like a security net for us overthinkers, but as overthinkers, we might worry about who is trust-worthy or not. The last thing we want is to confide in a friend about having a phobia of alarm clocks, and then they buy you one for your birthday. There is nothing worse than gossip sluts. Let's not let our overthinking imagination overwhelm or discourage us from reaching out to others when we need it most. If you are unsure who to allow into your inner social support circle, you can focus on building one instead. We aren't in high school anymore; we don't have to hang out with the cool kids to be cool or the goth kids to be noncon-forming. Before working on who's in and who's out, the different types of support systems are worth noting.

- **Emotional support systems.** Made up of non-judgmental close people who offer genuine advice and have your best interests at heart.
- **Social support systems.** While not as close, these people within your community positively influence or impact your life.
- **Professional support systems.** These people from your job or school typically help you achieve your goals.

Deciding the people you need in your life is challenging, especially if you were a past people pleaser or had terrible experiences entrusting others before. You can nurture a healthy support system with the following steps:

1- Figure out who is a healthy support for your life.
Sit down and make a list of people with whom you feel are vouching for you. Think about friends, family, acquaintances, and counselors. Once you have compiled the list, ask yourself probing questions such as:

- Do I trust them?
- Do they respect me?
- Do they help to bring out my best qualities?
- Can they make me cry with laughter by spinning a problem I had on its head, and then I realize how silly I have been?

If your answer is hell yes, it's time for the next step.

2- Communicate more.

Thanks to our technological age, there are many helpful resources to stay connected with people who matter the most to us. Maybe you've lost touch with a dear friend or are now developing a budding relationship with someone who gets you. Strengthen the bond proactively by:

- Staying connected through phone calls, emails, texts, zoom, or whatever you prefer.
- Telling them how important they are to your life.
- Offering them the opportunity to confide in you when they struggle.
- Accepting help when you need it.

3- Embrace shared interests.

Regular interactions are among the most remarkable ways to build relationships and connections. If you don't have existing friends or family for support, find the people who do through shared interests and hobbies. You can find like-minded people within your community, people you can connect with and ultimately confide in in various ways. I can't stress enough how much finding my people through the business Instagram account I started in April 2023 positively impacted my life. Once I committed to engaging actively with others there, I realized quickly that my story was not unique and that so many folks worldwide were starving for connection and the relief of feeling seen and understood. Consider activities such as:

- Volunteering
- Joining social media groups/following accounts based on your hobbies and interests (Inserting shameless plug here to encourage you to follow my Instagram account @sarcrasstic.self.care right now for ADHD community, punk attitude and empowerment, and neurodiverse humor if you don't already. I guarantee you will learn, laugh, and find at least some of your people. They're out there. I promise.)
- Attend classes in the gym or community centers.
- Invite people to social events such as concerts or open mic nights.
- Invite people to go on hikes or walks.

These all seem obvious, but they are easier said than done. If I took my own advice, I wouldn't have time for work between all the hikes, walks, gym workouts, concerts, etc. I'd probably also be ripped, so perhaps I should find a way to have endless cash so I never have to work again! But I digress. Again.

4- Be your own support system.
If you are introverted or shy, it's sometimes easier to look after yourself and not rely on anyone else. With some positive self-talk, self-care, and self-reflection, we can sometimes navi-

gate out of a difficult situation or crisis. Being a support system for yourself doesn't imply isolating yourself from others but taking responsibility for your well-being and looking after yourself. After a heavy night of partying, you might nurse your hangover with a movie and food. You should also give yourself the same level of self-care when you get overwhelmed.

Frequently, I have found that I could handle my over-thinking and anxiety through a myriad of ways. But life can sometimes make shit so hard that all your coping mecha-nisms fly out the window, and you begin overthinking to the point that it's dangerous. But how do you know when it's so bad? How do you know when your anxiety is so fucking out of control and your overthinking is so intense that you feel like nothing can help you?

You are not alone. I speak from personal experience here. When I got divorced and dealt with issues with work and my health, I was so overwhelmed that I had no idea what to do or where to go. Venting to the few people to whom I felt close enough didn't shift my perspective. Talking to the ghosts of my dead grandparents never helped either. So, how do you know when enough is enough?

If you think that maybe things are getting too much and that even your support system can't help, let alone anything else you tried, it may be time to seek help. Some signs to watch out for include the following:

- **Your anxiety or overthinking is affecting you physically.** We discussed before how overthinking or anxiety can cause so much mental stress that you struggle with sleep, but it can also cause digestive issues and unexplained muscle aches as well. You can feel as though all the energy has been sapped out of you, and you have little to no interest in eating. I've been there. I am 5′ 7″ tall (that's about 1m 71 for all my metric system folks… basically, the rest of the entire world) and I weighed 105 lbs (a frightening 47.75 kilos) in the summer of 2011. I. Have. Been. There.

- **Your anxiety comes from multiple sources.** It's tough when there is one big problem to deal with, but when multiple sources are causing you excessive worry, it can get far too overwhelming to the point that you can't concentrate or focus on anything. Some call it Murphy's Law, meaning anything that can go wrong will go wrong, be it with work, school, relationships, family, or your health.

- **Symptoms have persisted for at least six months.** Having occasional feelings of anxiety is still manageable, and more often than not, we can find some way to deal with it. It's when the symptoms have lingered with us for months that we need to consider doing something about it, as it's likely you've already tried to manage it, but nothing is working.

- **Your daily life is significantly impacted.** One of the most significant indicators that your anxiety and overthinking have reached critical levels is that it's impacting your everyday life. Your feelings of dread, fear, and worry can cause you significant distress and leave you like a shell of your former self. You struggle to function, isolate yourself, and feel like nobody or nothing will help.

- **You start abusing alcohol and drugs.** A big red flag for anxiety disorders is turning to unhealthy habits as coping mechanisms. Sure, the odd glass of wine can help you relax, but having several glasses every night can be a sign that you can't manage independently anymore. Many people often get addicted to their evening drinks to wind down after work, as well as to over-the-counter and prescription medications to help with sleep. If this is you (because it has been me), it may be time to seek help. Substance abuse can only further worsen symptoms of anxiety and stress, creating a vicious cycle of hopelessness that's hard to break.

If you feel like you are heading toward a downward spiral, don't assume you can't do anything about it. When I felt at rock bottom, I knew deep down that the only way was up (as cliché as it sounds, it's still very accurate). At one point in my life, I was dealing with so many things at the same time: divorce, raising kids, working my ass off at my job, and often feeling like I was more of a mom to my students than my own kids, as they would sometimes unload all their stress on me in my office hours, and occasionally even piles of other awful real and very traumatic shit with me being the first person they told said traumatic shit to, such that I was ready to lose my mind completely. Throw in undiagnosed ADHD and perimenopause, and that's a recipe for a category five shit storm hurricane. I needed help I couldn't give myself or get from my support groups. I needed a professional, and I am glad I found the courage to go back to therapy.

Seeking a therapist is nothing to be ashamed of. A lot of people have had one; even therapists have therapists. A therapist can help restore a relationship, adjust to a new area in your life, recover from past traumas, or help to improve your mental health. Finding the right therapist is challenging, as you want someone who can understand and relate to you. So here are a few suggestions to help you:

. . .

1- Look into various types of therapy first.

Therapy isn't just lying on a couch and venting to someone making notes. Many different kinds of treatment exist, so you want to pick one that aligns with what you hope to achieve. The following isn't an exhaustive list by a long shot, and these won't suit everyone. Furthermore, many of us need medication, but if you don't have a specific diagnosis, these therapies are fairly common practice and may offer a helpful point of departure. Remember: I am not a therapist/qualified professional. I provide these options as a baseline of discovery for those who have never gone to therapy. They are based on my lived experience and examples of therapies I have undergone:

- **Cognitive Behavioral Therapy (CBT)** is a therapeutic approach focusing on the connection between our thoughts, feelings, and behaviors. It helps identify and challenge negative or irrational thoughts and self-limiting beliefs that contribute to our stress and anxiety.
- **Acceptance and Commitment Therapy (ACT)** is a type of psychotherapy that combines mindfulness techniques with strategies to accept and embrace difficult emotions and experiences. As the name suggests, acceptance plays a key role, as does being present in the current moment instead of trying to eliminate or avoid the distressing thoughts or feelings plaguing us. ACT helps people clarify their values and commit to action, even in discomfort or challenges.
- **Dialectical Behavior Therapy (DBT)** is a comprehensive therapy initially developed for people with borderline personality disorder but is now adapted for other conditions as well. DBT

integrates cognitive-behavioral techniques with concepts from mindfulness and acceptance-based approaches. It's ideal for dealing with intense emotions, regulating emotions, or developing healthy coping strategies for self-sabotaging or self-destructive behaviors.

- **Psychoanalytic Therapy** was first developed by Sigmund Freud, with the main aim of this therapeutic approach being to explore our unconscious mind and its influence on behavior and mental health. This therapy delves into the importance of early childhood experiences and their effects on our unconscious desires and defense mechanisms. The therapist and client work together to uncover unconscious thoughts and emotions through dream analysis, free association, and other methods.

2- Know your budget.

One of the reasons people don't seek therapy is money, though you have to remember that you are investing in yourself just as much as they are investing in you. If you have insurance, check and see what it covers and determine how much you would be willing to pay for therapy. Knowing how much money you could set aside for a therapist can help prioritize the ones that work for your budget.

3- Ask someone you trust.

A referral from a friend, relative, colleague, or doctor you trust is a great way to find a therapist. You can get a much better insight into a therapist, especially if it's someone they have used themselves. Of course, the right therapist is dependent on your needs and goals more than anything.

4- Study the therapist's credentials.

When assessing a future therapist, it's good to check their credentials, such as specializing in a type of therapy you want to try or that is better for you. Then again, you can also find counselors, psychologists, or social workers experienced in a particular type of therapy.

5- Define your therapy goals ahead of time.

When you go to therapy, what do you hope to accomplish? To overcome anxiety? To deal with past trauma? To deal with overwhelming stress when shit has hit the fan? Preparing yourself to define your goals can make working with your therapist easier. If you suffer from specific symptoms, such as insomnia, your therapist can help you with medication. If you struggle with many issues, make a list and go through each thing. Your goals may change as you progress, and it's okay to talk to your therapist about this; you don't need to have goals beforehand, but it will help if you can.

6- Don't be afraid to ask them questions.

Finding a therapist for the first time is nerve-racking, especially after years of overthinking and anxiety. However, make things easier for yourself by asking them probing questions. Consider asking questions such as:

- What are your areas of expertise?
- What kind of therapy do you practice?

- Do you have experience working with clients in similar situations?
- How many years have you been practicing as a therapist?
- Am I going cuckoo or not?

7- Don't be afraid to try different therapists.

Finding the right therapist can involve trial and error (though you may luck out on your first try). Trying out a few therapists is normal, and once you have one that clicks with you, it's beneficial for you in the long run as you build rapport and develop a relationship.

8- Try online therapy.

Not everyone wants to discuss their issues face-to-face with strangers; they may be introverted and find it easier to seek online therapy. Finding online treatment has never been more accessible, so long as you have the financial means; for example, the website BetterHelp.com is highly regarded as a go-to for online therapy. It's still essential to check what your potential therapist specializes in and that they can meet your needs. Online therapy apps are also available, making it easier to leave a therapist and find a new one. I can't imagine anything more frustrating than telling a therapist face-to-face that you want to leave them, only for them to ask you probing questions about why (and still charge you).

Having a support system, especially as an overthinker with anxiety or as an anxiety-driven overthinker, can give us hope when we have tried everything else. If we don't have an immediate team of supporters in our corner, we can work on building one, and if we are too worried about sharing our problems, we can pay someone to listen instead. But in all seriousness, if you have made it this far in the book, it's evident that you want to make positive changes in your life proactively. By getting this book, you are taking action, and when you are overthinking or stressed AF, you have the can-do attitude to take further action, too.

If all else fails and you need to see a therapist, remember that it's not a sign of weakness but a sign of strength and bravery. To have that self-talk with yourself and say, "shit has hit the fan, and I need to talk to someone who might have the answers," is healthy and good. We can only do so much on our own, and while we hope that we can, if things get too much, then we must reach out. Life is not permanent, so don't take it seriously. Find humor in all the chaos; sometimes, that is enough and exactly what we need.

———

Key takeaway: Having a support system is essential.

CONCLUSION

"I TRIED to come up with a snarky and clever subtitle for this last chapter, but my brain is really tired after unloading all this knowledge, emotion, and humor on you. So, you get this 'quote' about how I wanted to have a funny subtitle but decided not to overthink it and let it go instead." — Sara Toninstan

But seriously. I am admittedly a little sad. We have finally reached the end of this book (which is a significant victory for us overthinkers as we usually struggle to finish anything), and I am going to miss you. I hope you enjoyed this humorous adventure as much as I did in writing it. Ideally, you are now empowered enough to overcome, or at least manage a little better, your overthinking and anxiety by finding your inner comedian. We've covered so much, but in case you need a reminder (I see you, my fellow ADHDers who read a sentence five times and still don't know what it said), or you were impatient, wanted to get to the point, and jumped straight from the intro to here (I still love you), here is a quick recap:

- In the first chapter, we looked at the science behind laughter, how it can improve mental resilience, overcome overthinking, cope with stress, improve communication, and help find common ground. Laughter has short-term perks, such as relief from stress and tension, muscle relaxation, and burning a few calories. Our brains reward us with releasing happy hormones such as dopamine and serotonin. Laughing regularly is even better, with improved lung and cognitive function and helping with inflammation. And the best thing is laughing is free.
- In the second chapter, we looked into the benefits of quitting overthinking by looking into why we struggle to quit anything in the first place due to habits or fear of change. By quitting overthinking, we can welcome with open arms benefits like better sleep, better relationships, and getting shit done. We also looked into ways to recognize when we are overthinking too much while also knowing that in moderation, it can be good.
- Chapter three was about delving into ways to let go of negative thoughts, focusing on how negative bias can play a significant role, such as giving more importance to negative experiences than positive ones and remembering insults more than praise. We also included a list of actionable strategies to deal with negative thoughts, such as hanging out with a pet or using a trash journal. Finally, we cover ways to embrace uncertainty, and that certainty is a natural part of life and it can provide us with opportunities for growth and learning.
- Chapter four is all about setting realistic goals and expectations, with some benefits including

motivating yourself, building confidence, and measuring progress. We distinguished the difference between unrealistic and realistic. We focused on the SMART (Specific, Measurable, Attainable, Relevant, and Time-bound) method of setting goals, which shows us that setting a goal is more complex than we initially thought.

- Chapter five is where we find out what anxiety and overthinking attacks are and how they can be triggered by things such as stress, phobias, and even caffeine. Some of the physical symptoms of an attack can include sweating, trembling, and shortness of breath. We discussed several techniques, such as taking deep breaths and avoiding triggers, to help when you feel an attack approaching. I also introduced a very wacky method of dealing with an attack by making up a ridiculous situation through observations around you. Alternatively, you can find solace by watching funny movies or listening to funny podcasts.

- Chapter six is all about cultivating a growth mindset. We compare the differences between a fixed mindset and a growth mindset. A growth mindset gives you the perspective to see challenges as opportunities and put more emphasis and passion on learning. Allowing mistakes to motivate you is the mantra here, and we go through methods to develop a growth mindset after learning of its incredible benefits.

- Chapter seven focuses on the power of self-deprecating humor and how it can help alleviate anxiety. Self-deprecating humor can also allow us to develop a growth mindset by gaining a fresh perspective and breaking the cycle of perfectionism (because making fun of ourselves means we aren't taking ourselves seriously anymore). The power of self-deprecating positive affirmations is also highlighted by using them when facing a challenge or feeling stressed.

- Chapter eight focuses on funny but encouraging ways to get more into physical activity, such as hula hooping or trampolining. The benefits of exercise (or any kind of physical activity for that matter) for mental health, such as boosting your mood and minimizing stress, are explored. You don't need to be a gym buff; you must get moving.

- Chapter nine is the last chapter about support systems and their importance when nothing else helps with your overthinking and anxiety. This chapter also highlights how to build a support system. This chapter also covers the importance of seeking professional help by looking into the signs that things have gotten too much, such as when you are overwhelmed by many different things at once in life. Seeking therapy is as healthy as finding the right therapist, with a step-by-step guide on choosing the right therapist for your needs and wants.

Deep breaths, everyone. This has been a rollercoaster to write (and I am sure to read, too!) I wrote this book because I found ways to manage my overthinking and anxiety through humor. I got married so young and realized after 20 years that I was unhappy, but I thought, "eff this," and quit my job, my marriage, and eventually, my old way of thinking. I achieved more goals than a Brazilian soccer team when I started working on myself *more intentionally* with humor. I was seeing the funny side of things I always took too seriously.

For me, humor has always been the ultimate coping mechanism. It helps strengthen relationships, gives me a better perspective on life, distracts me from my own thoughts, and, most importantly, helps me overcome so many things that I always thought I couldn't. My inner comedian has always been there, but it got a little lost the older I got. If you've lost yours as well, get your ass over to the Lost and Found and reunite! If you think you've never had an inner comedian, I challenge you to challenge that assumption! It's in there. Perhaps it's hiding, but it's definitely in there, and it's time to take it out of the cellar of your overthinking brain, dust it off, and go on a first date! Looking back, I can see how mine got buried, but like most things in life, with a bit of effort, I was able to pull her from the ashes of the trashcan fire that was my life at one point and relearn to harness humor's power. Sometimes, laughter is the best medicine; I hope this book proves that.

If you enjoyed this book and can utilize some of its many tips, tricks, and lessons, please be a total legend and consider leaving a positive review. Leaving a review will help to get my message out there to more overthinkers, and it's good karma, too!

EPILOGUE

MARCH 2024

Dear Badass Readers,

Hopefully you're on your way to being recovering over-thinkers now. As I read this book for the 83rd time and ditch all advice given therein about letting go of perfectionism, I find myself amazed at what I have accomplished. My imposter syndrome (whom I lovingly call Fiona) still looms and lurks in dark corners, and no matter how often I am able to lock her in a closet, she still manages to escape and taunt me. But I am proud of myself for finally getting this book done and flinging it into the ether, hoping that the folks who find it will get joy and solace from it.

Nevertheless, so much has changed in my life since I finally began to write this book almost exactly one year ago: For starters, *I left my life-long career as a college professor* (and sadly some awesome colleagues with it). I was perpetually stressed out and something had to give. It was not an easy decision. I spent most of my adult life in graduate school and then working in higher education, so the shift was massive.

But for me, the change was worth it. I began pursuing and creating my own entrepreneurial opportunities that fuel my creativity and align with my values, and I am exponentially less stressed out. My mental health is thanking me.

I began to write outside of academia again. First and foremost, I am writing books that focus on mental health through the lens of humor. Even though this book is not a novel, not fiction, all writing constitutes creative writing for me. It is a deeply personal and creative process, and I poured my heart, soul, full sass and humor into the writing of this book to make a non-fiction "self-help" book as fun, creative, and funny as possible.

That said, *I decided to publish these books under a pen name.* Here's why: My real name is Sarah Glasco. Authors often choose pen names to hide. They don't want their true identity exposed for various reasons. For me it's as simple as this: I've been a published academic author for a long time, and honestly, I think adding titles from this new genre to my list of previous scholarly publications, which are very different, would be confusing for the algorithms and potential future readers. That's all.

Regardless, I want people to know who I really am because I am just a regular, vulnerable human being with a very messy house, and bills to pay, and real raw human emotions; a divorced mom trying to succeed in life, a "normal" person who wants to do good and be kind, but who still sometimes fucks up ... because I'm human and life is hard sometimes. Yeah.

To make things even more interesting... *I discovered I had ADHD and sought and received formal diagnosis.* This knowledge in and of itself has been life-changing for me and transformative in terms of my own self-acceptance in a way almost too profound to articulate. Formal diagnosis is a privilege. Not everyone has access to it. That said, self-diagnosis is valid. However, if you think there's something "wrong" with you, if you suspect you might have a diagnosable disorder or a mental health condition that medical intervention could help, I encourage you to reach out to someone you trust, seek out resources, and make an appointment with a doctor, mental health professional, or therapist to see what your options are and what next steps to take. It could change your life. *I did go back to therapy after a year off to start unpacking all the baggage and unraveling the tangled threads that inevitably come with a late-in-life ADHD diagnosis.* I didn't know I had ADHD when I started writing this book, and that perspective shift has ultimately been a blessing in disguise for this and future books as well as all the relationships in my life.

All the while, *my dad fell very ill and passed away in September.* If you've ever lost anything or anyone you love, you've grieved. Grief isn't just about death. It's about loss. Grief is an extension & expression of love. Grief is an inevitable part of the human experience. When I quit my job last year and told my dad I was going to start my own company, be my own boss, and write full-time, he didn't flinch. He didn't question me. Not even for a second. If anything, I think he was genuinely impressed. He trusted and supported me, and his response was the embodiment of what a strong support system looks like and how privileged I am to have had that in both my parents.

In less than one year, *I have met so many people from around the world on Instagram in the mental health and ADHD communities* via my @sarcrasstic.self.care account, and I've grown to love, respect, and really lean on these beautiful souls when I am feeling not only fragile, frustrated, or frightened, but also excited, silly, hopeful, and happy.

And most recently, *I started medication for ADHD* and am tapering off the SSRI I had been taking for anxiety for years. And guess, what? Suddenly my brain is less chaotic. My anxiety is melting away, and I'm stunned at how much it is helping me. This may be the missing piece of my neurological puzzle.

So you see, a lot can change in the span of year. You just don't know. Finding out I had ADHD in particular, subsequently peeling off all the masks I had been wearing in some way or another my entire life, and stopping guilting myself about perceived failures and my inability to just simply get shit done on a neurotypical world's timeline and trajectory has been astonishingly freeing. I am grateful for this new knowledge and am so glad to have you on this trip with me.

―――――

Onward! Onward to the next
Sarcrasstic Self Care book!
See you there.
Love,
Sara(h)

―――――

SOURCES CONSULTED AND/OR CITED

Also known as the Bibliography, the Science, the Evidence, the Facts, or better yet, "Damn, look how much research I did for this book!"

SCHOLARLY ARTICLES AND BOOKS

Akimbekov, N. S., & Razzaque, M. S. (2021). Laughter therapy: A humor-induced hormonal intervention to reduce stress and anxiety. *Current Research in Physiology*, 4, 135–138. https://doi.org/10.1016/j.crphys.2021.04.002

Bachorowski, J. A., & Owren, M. J. (2001). Not all laughs are alike: voiced but not unvoiced laughter readily elicits positive affect. *Psychological science*, 12(3), 252–257. https://doi.org/10.1111/1467-9280.00346

Bains, G. S., Berk, L. S., Lohman, E., Daher, N., Petrofsky, J., Schwab, E., & Deshpande, P. (2015). Humors Effect on Short-term Memory in Healthy and Diabetic Older Adults. *Alternative therapies in health and medicine*, 21(3), 16–25.

Bega, D., Palmentera, P., Wagner, A., Hovde, M., Barish, B., Kwasny, M. J., & Simuni, T. (2017). Laughter is the best medicine: The Second City® improvisation as an intervention for Parkinson's disease. *Parkinsonism & related disorders*, 34, 62–65. https://doi.org/10.1016/j.parkreldis.2016.11.001

Bennett, M. P., & Lengacher, C. (2009). Humor and Laughter May Influence Health IV. Humor and Immune Function. *Evidence-based complementary and alternative medicine : eCAM*, 6(2), 159–164. https://doi.org/10.1093/ecam/nem149

Berk, L. S., Felten, D. L., Tan, S. A., Bittman, B. B., & Westengard, J. (2001). Modulation of neuroimmune parameters during the eustress of humor-associated mirthful laughter. *Alternative therapies in health and medicine*, 7(2), 62–76.

Buchowski, M. S., Majchrzak, K. M., Blomquist, K., Chen, K. Y., Byrne, D. W., & Bachorowski, J. A. (2005). Energy expenditure of genuine laughter. *International journal of obesity*, 31(1), 131–137. https://doi.org/10.1038/sj.ijo.0803353

Cai, C., Yu, L., Rong, L., & Zhong, H. (2014). Effectiveness of humor intervention for patients with schizophrenia: a randomized controlled trial. *Journal of psychiatric research*, 59, 174–178. https://doi.org/10.1016/j.jpsychires.2014.09.010

Curry, O., & Dunbar, R. I. M. (2013). Sharing a joke: the effects of a similar sense of humor on affiliation and altruism. *Evolution and Human Behavior, 34*, 125–129. https://doi.org/10.1016/j.evolhumbehav.2012.11.003

Dezecache, G., & Dunbar, R. I. M. (2012). Sharing the joke: The size of natural laughter groups. *Evolution and Human Behavior, 33*(6), 775–77. https://doi.org/10.1016/j.evolhumbehav.2012.07.002

Dunbar, R.I.M., Launay, J. & Curry, O. The Complexity of Jokes Is Limited by Cognitive Constraints on Mentalizing. *Hum Nat* 27, 130–140 (2016). https://doi.org/10.1007/s12110-015-9251-6

Dunbar, R. I., Baron, R., Frangou, A., Pearce, E., van Leeuwen, E. J., Stow, J., Partridge, G., MacDonald, I., Barra, V., & van Vugt, M. (2012). Social laughter is correlated with an elevated pain threshold. *Proceedings. Biological sciences, 279*(1731), 1161–1167. https://doi.org/10.1098/rspb.2011.1373

Dunbar, R. I., Marriott, A., & Duncan, N. D. (1997). Human conversational behavior. *Human nature (Hawthorne, N.Y.), 8*(3), 231–246. https://doi.org/10.1007/BF02912493

Flamson, T., & Barrett, H. C. (2008). The encryption theory of humor: A knowledge-based mechanism of honest signaling. *Journal of Evolutionary Psychology, 6*(4), 261–281. https://doi.org/10.1556/JEP.6.2008.4.2

Grammer, K. (1990). Strangers meet: Laughter and nonverbal signs of interest in opposite-sex encounters. *Journal of Nonverbal Behavior, 14*(4), 209–236. https://doi.org/10.1007/BF00989317

Grav, S., Hellzèn, O., Romild, U. and Stordal, E. (2012), Association between social support and depression in the general population: the HUNT study, a cross-sectional survey. *Journal of Clinical Nursing, 21:* 111-120. https://doi.org/10.1111/j.1365-2702.2011.03868.x

Hanson, R. (2013). *Hardwiring Happiness: The New Brain Science of Contentment, Calm, and Confidence.* First edition. New York, Harmony Books.

James, K. A., Stromin, J. I., Steenkamp, N., & Combrinck, M. I. (2023). Understanding the relationships between physiological and psychosocial stress, cortisol and cognition. *Frontiers in Endocrinology, 14*, 1085950. https://doi.org/10.3389/fendo.2023.1085950

Jellinek, M. (2010). Don't Let ADHD Crush Children's Self-Esteem. *Clinical Psychiatry News. 38.* 12. 10.1016/S0270-6644(10)70231-9.

Kafle, E., Papastavrou Brooks, C., Chawner, D., Foye, U., Declercq, D., & Brooks, H. (2023). "Beyond laughter": A systematic review to understand how interventions utilise comedy for individuals experiencing mental health problems. *Frontiers in Psychology, 14*, 1161703. https://doi.org/10.3389/fpsyg.2023.1161703

Larion, K. S. (2014). Technology Based Mental Health Support Strategies for Youth. *Electronic Thesis and Dissertation Repository.* 1924. https://ir.lib.uwo.ca/etd/1924

Lee, J. Y., Slater, M. D., & Tchernev, J. (2015). Self-Deprecating Humor Versus Other-Deprecating Humor in Health Messages. *Journal of health communication, 20*(10), 1185–1195. https://doi.org/10.1080/10810730.2015.1018591

Li, N. P., Griskevicius, V., Durante, K. M., Jonason, P. K., Pasisz, D. J., & Aumer, K. (2009). An evolutionary perspective on humor: Sexual selection or interest indication? *Personality and Social Psychology Bulletin, 35*(7), 923–936. https://doi.org/10.1177/0146167209334786

Lopes-Júnior, L. C., Bomfim, E., Olson, K., Neves, E. T., Silveira, D. S. C., Nunes, M. D. R., Nascimento, L. C., Pereira-da-Silva, G., & Lima, R. A. G. (2020). Effectiveness of hospital clowns for symptom management in paediatrics: systematic review of randomised and non-randomised controlled trials. *BMJ (Clinical research ed.), 371*, m4290. https://doi.org/10.1136/bmj.m4290

Low, L. F., Goodenough, B., Fletcher, J., Xu, K., Casey, A. N., Chenoweth, L., Fleming, R., Spitzer, P., Bell, J. P., & Brodaty, H. (2014). The effects of humor therapy on nursing home residents measured using observational methods: the SMILE cluster randomized trial. *Journal of the American Medical Directors Association, 15*(8), 564–569. https://doi.org/10.1016/j.jamda.2014.03.017

Manninen, S., Tuominen, L., Dunbar, R. I., Karjalainen, T., Hirvonen, J., Arponen, E., Hari, R., Jääskeläinen, I. P., Sams, M., & Nummenmaa, L. (2017). Social Laughter Triggers Endogenous Opioid Release in Humans. *The Journal of neuroscience : the official journal of the Society for Neuroscience, 37*(25), 6125–6131. https://doi.org/10.1523/JNEUROSCI.0688-16.2017

McGrath, J. J., Al-Hamzawi, A., Alonso, J., Altwaijri, Y., Andrade, L. H., Bromet, E. J., Bruffaerts, R., de Almeida, J. M. C., Chardoul, S., Chiu, W. T., Degenhardt, L., Demler, O. V., Ferry, F., Gureje, O., Haro, J. M., Karam, E. G., Karam, G., Kessler, R.C., Khaled, S. M., Kovess-Masfety, V., Magno, M., Medina-Mora, M.E., Moskalewicz, J., Navarro-Mateu, F., Nishi, D., Plana-Ripoll, O., Posada-Villa, J., Rapsey, C., Sampson, N.A., Stagnaro, J.C., Stein, D. J., Have, M.T., Torres, Y., Vladescu, C., Woodruff, P.W., Zarkov, Z., WHO World Mental Health Survey Collaborators (2023). Age of onset and cumulative risk of mental disorders: a cross-national analysis of population surveys from 29 countries. *The Lancet. Psychiatry, 10*(9), 668–681. https://doi.org/10.1016/S2215-0366(23)00193-1

Meier, M., Wirz, L., Dickinson, P., & Pruessner, J. C. (2021). Laughter yoga reduces the cortisol response to acute stress in healthy individuals. *Stress (Amsterdam, Netherlands), 24*(1), 44–52. https://doi.org/10.1080/10253890.2020.1766018

Menéndez-Aller, Á., Postigo, Á., Montes-Álvarez, P., González-Primo, F. J., & García-Cueto, E. (2020). Humor as a protective factor against anxiety and depression. *International journal of clinical and health psychology : IJCHP,*

20(1), 38–45. https://doi.org/10.1016/j.ijchp.2019.12.002

Miller, M., & Fry, W. F. (2009). The effect of mirthful laughter on the human cardiovascular system. *Medical hypotheses*, 73(5), 636–639. https://doi.org/10.1016/j.mehy.2009.02.044

Mora-Ripoll R. (2010). The therapeutic value of laughter in medicine. *Alternative therapies in health and medicine*, 16(6), 56–64.

Nevo, O., Keinan, G., & Teshimovsky-Arditi, M. (1993). Humor and pain tolerance. *Humor: International Journal of Humor Research,* 6(1), 71–88. https://doi.org/10.1515/humr.1993.6.1.71

Oczkowski S. (2015). Virtuous laughter: we should teach medical learners the art of humor. *Critical care (London, England)*, 19(1), 222. https://doi.org/10.1186/s13054-015-0927-4

Owens, T. J., Stryker, S., & Goodman, N. (2006). Extending Self-Esteem Theory and Research: Sociological and Psychological Currents. Cambridge University Press. https://doi.org/10.1017/CBO9780511527739

Owens, T. J. (1993). Accentuate the Positive-and the Negative: Rethinking the Use of Self-Esteem, Self-Deprecation, and Self-Confidence. *Social Psychology Quarterly*, 56(4), 288–299. https://doi.org/10.2307/2786665

Panepinto, J. C. (2019, July 18). ADHD: Parenting Beyond Behavior, Beliefs, and Grades. *CHADD*. https://chadd.org/adhd-weekly/use-summer-to-improve-your-parent-child-relationship/

Provine, R. R. (2001). *Laughter: A scientific investigation*. Penguin Books.

Ramachandran V. S. (1998). The neurology and evolution of humor, laughter, and smiling: the false alarm theory. *Medical hypotheses*, 51(4), 351–354. https://doi.org/10.1016/s0306-9877(98)90061-5

Romundstad, S., Svebak, S., Holen, A., & Holmen, J. (2016). A 15-Year Follow-Up Study of Sense of Humor and Causes of Mortality: The Nord-Trøndelag Health Study. *Psychosomatic medicine*, 78(3), 345–353. https://doi.org/10.1097/PSY.0000000000000275

Savage, B. M., Lujan, H. L., Thipparthi, R. R., & DiCarlo, S. E. (2017). Humor, laughter, learning, and health! A brief review. *Advances in physiology education*, 41(3), 341–347. https://doi.org/10.1152/advan.00030.2017

Sherman, S. M., Cheng, Y. P., Fingerman, K. L., & Schnyer, D. M. (2016). Social support, stress and the aging brain. *Social Cognitive and Affective Neuroscience,* 11(7), 1050–1058. https://doi.org/10.1093/scan/nsv071

Speer, S. A. (2019). Reconsidering self-deprecation as a communication practice. *British Journal of Social Psychology*, 58(4), 806-828. https://bpspsychub.onlinelibrary.wiley.com/doi/abs/10.1111/bjso.12329

Torres-Marín, J., Navarro-Carrillo, G. & Carretero-Dios, H. (2017). Is the use of humor associated with anger management? The assessment of individual differences in humor styles in Spain. *Personality and Individual*

Differences. 120. 193-201. 10.1016/j.paid.2017.08.040.

Umberson, D., & Montez, J. K. (2010). Social relationships and health: a flash-point for health policy. *Journal of Health and Social Behavior*, 51 Suppl(Suppl), S54–S66. https://doi.org/10.1177/0022146510383501

AUTHORED BLOGS, WEB ARTICLES, VIDEOS & CONFERENCE PROCEEDINGS

Alvord, M., Uchino, B., & Wright, V. (2019, October 8). Manage stress: Strengthen your support network. *American Psychological Association.* https://www.apa.org/topics/stress/manage-social-support

Barkley, S. (2022, October 28). Self Expectations: 7 Suggestions for Setting Realistic Expectations. *Psych Central.* https://psychcentral.com/health/suggestions-for-setting-realistic-expectations-with-yourself

Bansal, V. (n.d.). 5 Strategies to Stop Overthinking and Start Acting. *Tech Tello.* https://www.techtello.com/stop-overthinking/

Barr, S. (2018, February 13). Self-deprecating humor linked to psychological wellbeing, study finds. *Independent.* https://www.independent.co.uk/life-style/health-and-families/self-deprecating-humour-greater-psychological-wellbeing-link-study-university-of-granada-spain-a8207976.html

Barrell, R. (2016, July 1). How Laughter And Comedy Can Help With Depression, Anxiety And Other Mental Illnesses. *HuffPost.* https://www.huffingtonpost.co.uk/entry/the-best-medicine_uk_57702a73e4b0232d331e3262

Blackman, T. K. (n.d.). 10 tips to building a support system. *T. Kea Blackman.* https://www.t-keablackman.com/post/10-tips-to-building-a-support-system

Boyer, A. (2021, June 8). 9 Signs You're Overthinking Something. *Introvert, Dear. https://introvertdear.com/news/9-signs-youre-overthinking-something/*

Brandt, A., Ph.D. (2019, March 1). 6 Signs It's Time to Seek Help for Your Anxiety. *Psychology Today.* https://www.psychologytoday.com/us/blog/mindful-anger/201903/6-signs-it-s-time-seek-help-your-anxiety

Bryan, J. (2015, July 6). One key difference in math achievement: Jason Bourne and entity orientation. *Renaissance.* https://www.renaissance.com/2015/07/06/one-key-difference-in-math-achievement-jason-bourne-and-entity-orientation/

Cann, P. (2020, November 18). Why are laughter and endorphins connected? *Canned Laughter.* https://petecann.com/laughter-and-endorphins/

Carter, C., Ph.D. (2020, October 21). 7 strategies to help you live with uncertainty. *IDEAS.TED.COM*. https://ideas.ted.com/7-strategies-to-help-you-live-with-uncertainty/

Chai, C. (2022, April 26). How to Find a Therapist Who's Right for You. *Everyday Health*. https://www.everydayhealth.com/emotional-health/how-to-find-a-therapist-whos-right-for-you/

Cheng, K. (2019, February 18). The Joke's On Me: The Benefits of Self Deprecating Humor. *Verde Magazine*. https://verdemagazine.com/the-jokes-on-me-the-benefits-of-self-deprecating-humor

Cherry, K. (2023, March 3). How Social Support Contributes to Psychological Health. *Verywell Mind*. https://www.verywellmind.com/social-support-for-psychological-health-4119970

Cherry, K. (2022, May 20). The Benefits of Making Fun of Yourself. *Verywell Mind*. https://www.verywellmind.com/the-benefits-of-making-fun-of-yourself-5271389

Chu, M. (2021, August 28.). 10 signs you're overthinking things. *Ladders*. https://www.theladders.com/career-advice/10-signs-youre-overthinking-things

Cohan, P. (2021, January 29). 4 ways to embrace uncertainty and ambiguity. *Inc*. https://www.inc.com/peter-cohan/4-ways-to-embrace-uncertainty-ambiguity.html

Davila, J., Ph.D. (2016, June 17). Stop Trying to Fix Things, Just Listen! ["Sometimes it's not about finding a solution but finding someone who understands your problem." -Unknown] *Psychology Today*. https://www.psychologytoday.com/us/blog/skills-healthy-relationships/201606/stop-trying-fix-things-just-listen

Davis, T., Ph.D. (2019, April 11). 15 ways to Build a Growth Mindset. *Psychology Today*. https://www.psychologytoday.com/us/blog/click-here-happiness/201904/15-ways-build-growth-mindset

Deschene, L. (n.d.). 7 Ways to Deal with Uncertainty So You Can Be Happy and Less Anxious. *Tiny Buddha*. https://tinybuddha.com/blog/7-ways-to-deal-with-uncertainty/

Deschene, L. (n.d.). 40 Ways to Let Go and Feel Less Pain. *Tiny Buddha*. https://tinybuddha.com/blog/40-ways-to-let-go-and-feel-less-pain/

Dodson, W. W. (2022, May 2). How ADHD Shapes Your Perceptions, Emotions & Motivation. *adhd.dk*. https://adhd.dk/wp-content/uploads/sites/2/2022/05/Dodson-How-ADHD-Shapes-Your-Perceptions-Emotions-.pdf

Dorter, G. (n.d.). Letting Go of Thoughts Mindfully. *Guelph Therapist*. https://www.guelphtherapist.ca/blog/letting-go-of-thoughts-mindfully/

Dweck, C. (2015, September 23). Carol Dweck Revisits the 'Growth Mindset'. *Education Week. Ed Week*. http://www.edweek.org/ew/articles/2015/09/23/carol-dweck-revisits-the-growth-mindset.html?cmp=cpc-goog-ew-

growth+mindset&ccid=growth+mindset&ccag=growth+mindset&
cckw=%2Bgrowth%20%2Bmindset&cccv=content+ad&gclid=Cj0KEQiAn
vfDBRCXrabLl6-6t-0BEiQAW4SRUM7nekFnoTxc675qBMSJycFgwERo
hguZWVmNDcSUg5gaAk3I8P8HAQ

Dweck, C. (2014, November). The power of believing that you can improve.
[Video]. *TED.* https://www.ted.com/talks/carol_dweck_the_power_of_
believing_that_you_can_improve?language=en

Fahkry, T. (2018, March 30). How To Embrace And Get Comfortable With
Uncertainty In Life. *Medium.* https://medium.com/the-mission/how-to-
embrace-and-get-comfortable-with-uncertainty-in-life-9716a1633182

Foreman, A. & Rosenberg, A. (2022, April 17). 27 funniest Netflix stand-up
specials to laugh your butt off to. *Mashable.* https://sea.mashable.com/
entertainment/9630/the-24-funniest-stand-up-specials-to-watch-on-
netflix-while-social-distancing

Freeman, L. (2017, March 1). Mental fitness: Study shows seniors stay
healthier with social connections. *Naples News.* https://www.naplesnews.
com/story/news/2017/03/01/mental-fitness-study-shows-seniors-stay-
healthier-social-connections/98520962/

Fuller, R. &Shikaloff, N. (2016, December 14). What Great Managers Do Daily.
Harvard Business Review. https://hbr.org/2016/12/what-great-managers-
do-daily

Gaille, B. (2015, September 25). 8 pros and cons of overthinking. *Brandon-
Gaille: Small Business & Marketing Advice.* https://brandongaille.com/8-
pros-and-cons-of-overthinking/

Gastelum, J. (2021, January 20). Why Our Brains Fixate on the Bad (and What
to Do About It) *Lexipol Wellness.* https://www.cordico.com/2021/01/20/
why-our-brains-fixate-on-the-bad-and-what-to-do-about-
it/#:~:text=Our%20brains%20have%20been%20hardwired,and%20-
passed%20on%20their%20genes.

Gherini, A. (2018, November 29). What a self-deprecating sense of humor
says about your EQ. *Inc.* https://www.inc.com/anne-gherini/what-a-
self-deprecating-sense-of-humor-says-about-your-eq.html

Griggs, B. (2020, January 15). Using Humor as a Coping Tool. *National
Alliance on Mental Illness.* https://www.nami.org/Blogs/NAMI-Blog/
January-2020/Using-Humor-as-a-Coping-Tool

Hernandez-Santana, A. (2022, September 14). HERC associate director: Ways
to stay grounded. *Daily Eastern News.* https://core.ac.uk/download/
541431121.pdf

Hood, J., Ph.D. (2020, February 3). (n.d.). The Benefits And Importance Of A
Support System. *Highlands Springs Specialty Clinic.* https://highland
springsclinic.org/the-benefits-and-importance-of-a-support-system/

Hoyle, K. (2023, June 14). Supporting a Teenager with ADHD. *LinkedIn.*

https://www.linkedin.com/pulse/supporting-teenager-adhd-kate-hoyle

Hunt, K. (2021, July 1). The science of laughter and why it's good for us. *CNN.* https://www.cnn.com/2021/07/01/health/science-of-laughter-scn-wellness/index.html

Hutchinson, A. (2020, August 11). The importance of a good support system and how to find one. *Ovrcome* https://www.ovrcome.io/post/the-impor tance-of-a-good-support-system-and-how-to-find-one

Jha, N.A. (2019, August 30). Overthinking, good or bad? *Medium.* https://medium.com/@neha.anand.jha/does-overthinking-harm-you-b3bce f63c8ca

Journey, Sysy. (2019, October 7). I used to think that my life was a tragedy, but now I realize, it's a comedy. ["My overthinking is so advanced, it could write a bestselling novel – too bad it's a comedy about my life." – Unknown] *Medium.* https://medium.com/extraordinary-sysygarden/i-used-to-think-that-my-life-was-a-tragedy-but-now-i-realize-its-a-comedy-d973b3f79847

Kingma, A. (2022, June 1). 7 Signs You Are Overthinking and How It Can Negatively Affect Your Mental Health. *Mindfulness for Health.* https://mindfulnessforhealth.ca/blog/2022/06/01/7-signs-you-are-overthink ing-and-how-it-can-negatively-affect-your-mental-health

Koyama, S. (2023, February 27).How Community Matters for Your Mental Health. *Painted Brain.* https://paintedbrain.org/blog/mental-health/how-community-matters-for-your-mental-health

Kramer, G. (2022, June 6). Using self-deprecating humor as a coping mecha-nism. *Medium.* https://medium.com/@garyk/using-self-deprecating-humour-as-a-coping-mechanism-df67e5162962

Lamothe, C. (2018, June 22.). The Benefits of Laughing at Yourself According to Science. *Shondaland.* https://www.shondaland.com/live/a21755063/benefits-laughing-at-yourself-self-deprecation-science-psychology/

Lebow, H. I. (2021, June 7). How to Let Go of Negative Thoughts. *Psych Central.* https://psychcentral.com/depression/letting-go-of-negative-thoughts#step-back

Lindberg, S. (2023, March 21). How to Let Go of Things From the Past. *Healthline.* https://www.healthline.com/health/how-to-let-go

Lish, M. (n.d.). What If Your "Overthinking" Is Actually Good For You? *Tiny Buddha.* https://tinybuddha.com/blog/change-challenges-blog/what-if-your-overthinking-is-actually-good-for-you/

Lonczak, H.S., Ph.D. (2020, November 17). 36 Ways to Find a Silver Lining During Challenging Times. *Positive Psychology.* https://positivepsychol ogy.com/find-a-silver-lining/

Lyubomirsky, S., Ph.D., Reviewer. (n.d.) Create joy and satisfaction. *Mental Health America.* http://www.mentalhealthamerica.net/create-joy-and-satisfaction

McCallum, K. (2021, April 12). When Overthinking Becomes a Problem and What You Can Do About It. *Houston Methodist.* https://www.houston methodist.org/blog/articles/2021/apr/when-overthinking-becomes-a-problem-and-what-you-can-do-about-it/#:~:text=Signs%20that%20you%20might%20be,your%20mistakes%20in%20your%20mind

McGrath, N. (2021, September 25). How stand-up comedy helped me conquer anxiety, depression –and fear of public speaking. *The Guardian.* https://www.theguardian.com/lifeandstyle/2021/sep/25/how-standup-comedy-helped-me-conquer-anxiety-depression-and-fear-of-public-speaking

McNutt, C. (2023, January 2023). This is why we should stop giving home-work. *Human Restoration Project.* https://www.humanrestorationproject.org/writing/this-is-why-we-should-stop-giving-home work#:~:text=They%20found%20that%20time%20spent,Some%20stud-ies%20are%20more%20positive

Mehta, N. (2022, July 24). Signs That You Are An Overthinker. *My Fit Brain.* https://myfitbrain.in/blog/signs-that-you-are-an-overthinker

Morin, A. (2020, April 20). 10 signs you're overthinking and what to do about it. *Forbes.* https://www.forbes.com/sites/amymorin/2020/04/20/10-signs-youre-overthinking-and-what-to-do-about-it/?sh=6a2292d92bb8

Morin, A. (2019, January 7). 10 Signs You're an Overthinker: There's a big difference between ruminating and problem-solving. *Inc.* https://www.inc.com/amy-morin/10-signs-you-think-too-much-and-what-you-can-do-about-it.html

O'Malley, K. (2017). Is Your Self-Deprecating Sense of Humor Psychologically and Socially Damaging? *Elle Magazine.* https://www.elle.com/uk/life-and-culture/culture/longform/a35183/self-deprecation-humour-psycho logically-socially-damaging/

Oshea, D., Psy.D. (n.d.). You are not an island. *Dr. Deb's Emotional Wellness Blog.* https://www.droshea.com/blog/you-are-not-an-island

Patel, V. (n.d.). The Difference Between Humility and Self-Deprecation. *Vaishali Patel Psychotherapy. https://www.vaishalipatelpsychotherapy.com/differ ence-humility-self-deprecation/https://www.vaishalipatelpsychotherapy.com/ difference-humility-self-deprecation/*

Peterson, T.J. (2014, December 25). (2014, December). Laughter Can Chase Away Anxiety. *HealthyPlace.* https://www.healthyplace.com/blogs/anxi ety-schmanxiety/2014/12/laughter-can-chase-away-anxiety

Pike, M. (2019, August 27). When Does Self-Deprecating Humor Become

Detrimental? *Talkspace.* https://www.talkspace.com/blog/self-depreca
tion-unhealthy/

Plumptre, E. (2023, November 26). Self-Deprecation: Harmless Habit or
Unhealthy Behavior? *Verywell Mind.* https://www.verywellmind.com/
what-is-self-deprecation-5186918

Rapaport, L. (2023, November 16). What Does a Panic Attack Look and Feel
Like? *Everyday Health.*https://www.everydayhealth.com/conditions/
what-its-like-to-have-an-anxiety-attack/#:~:text=For%20doc-
tors%20to%20diagnose%20a,(heart%20palpita-
tions)%2C%20and%20feeling

Resnick, B. (2019, August 1). 22 percent of millennials say they have "No
friends". *Vox.* https://www.vox.com/science-and-health/2019/8/1/
20750047/millennials-poll-loneliness

Rindfleisch, J. A., MPhil, MD. (n.d.). The healing benefits of humor and
laughter. *Va.gov.* https://www.va.gov/WHOLEHEALTHLIBRARY/
tools/healing-benefits-humor-laughter.asp

Riordan, H. (2017, May 3). Overthinking Is Actually A Good Thing. *Thought
Catalog.* https://thoughtcatalog.com/holly-riordan/2017/05/overthink
ing-is-actually-a-good-thing/#:~:text=Your%20overthinking%20has%20-
turned%20you,You've%20thought%20everything%20through

Robinson, L. & Smith, M. (2024, February 5). Dealing with Uncertainty. *Help-
Guide.org.* https://www.helpguide.org/articles/anxiety/dealing-with-
uncertainty.htm

Santos, J. (n.d.). 30 funny & encouraging anxiety quotes that are WAY too
relatable. *Butfirstjoy.com.* https://butfirstjoy.com/encouraging-anxiety-
quotes/

Roundtable on Population Health Improvement; Board on Population Health
and Public Health Practice; Institute of Medicine. Business Engagement in
Building Healthy Communities: Workshop Summary. Washington (DC):
National Academies Press (US); 2015 May 8. 2, Lessons from the Blue
Zones®. https://www.ncbi.nlm.nih.gov/books/NBK298903/

Sasson, R. (n.d.). 6 Reasons Why You Need to Stop Overthinking. *Success
Consciousness.* https://www.successconsciousness.com/blog/mindful
ness/why-you-need-to-stop-overthinking/

Sharpe, R. (2020, October 7). 100+ Anxiety Quotes to Help You Feel Calmer.
[Me: "What could possibly go wrong?" My anxiety: "I'm glad you asked."
–Unknown] *Declutter the Mind.* https://declutterthemind.com/blog/anxi
ety-quotes/

Sharpe, R. (2020, October 7). 100+ Anxiety Quotes to Help You Feel Calmer.
["I came. I saw. I had anxiety. So I left." – Unknown] *Declutter the Mind.*
https://declutterthemind.com/blog/anxiety-quotes/

Smith, J. (2022, September 26). 30 Simple Ways to Free Your Mind Immediately. *LifeHack* https://www.lifehack.org/articles/communication/30-ways-free-your-mind-immediately.html

Sperber, Sarah. (n.d.). Overthinking: Definition, Causes, and How to Stop. *Berkeley Well-being Institute.* https://www.berkeleywellbeing.com/over thinking.html

Srini. (2021, June 7). Why Self-Deprecating Humor is More Good Than Bad For You. *Medium.* https://medium.com/feedium/why-self-deprecating-humor-is-more-good-than-bad-for-you-ef97009490d9

Stanborough, R. J. & Lee, M. (2024, March 15). How to Find a Therapist. 8 Tips for the Right Fit. *Healthline.* https://www.healthline.com/health/how-to-find-a-therapist

Styles, C. (2020, December 31). How to let things go. *Camille Styles.* https://camillestyles.com/wellness/how-to-let-things-go/

Travers, B. & Greene, S. (2023, February 24). The 75 Best TV Comedies of All Time. *IndieWire.* https://www.indiewire.com/feature/best-comedy-tv-shows-all-time-netflix-hbo-1202053555/

Tyagi, H. (2022, August 5). 60 Best Funny Anxiety Quotes to Calm Yourself. *The Quotes Flix.* https://www.thequotesflix.com/funny-anxiety-quotes/

Walsh, C. (2021, February 17). Young Adults Hardest Hit by Loneliness During Pandemic. *The Harvard Gazette.* https://news.harvard.edu/gazette/story/2021/02/young-adults-teens-loneliness-mental-health-coronavirus-covid-pandemic/

Weniger, K. (2022, April 4).How to Create a Strong Support System: 10 Tips. *Institute For Integrative Nutrition.* https://www.integrativenutrition.com/blog/creating-a-strong-support-system

Whiteman, H. (2017, June 3). Laughter releases 'feel good hormones' to promote social bonding. *Medical News Today.* https://www.medicalnew stoday.com/articles/317756

Willams, T., Ph.D. (n.d.). Mental Health Quotes: Short, Funny, & Inspirational. *Berkeley Well-being Institute.* https://www.berkeleywellbeing.com/mental-health-quotes.html

Witmer, S.A. (2023, March 24.). What is Overthinking, and How Do I Stop Overthinking Everything? *GoodRx Health..* https://www.goodrx.com/well-being/healthy-mind/how-can-i-stop-overthinking-everything

Wooll, M. (2021, July 26). 13 tips to develop a growth mindset. *BetterUp.* https://www.betterup.com/blog/growth-mindset

Yang, S. (2021, January 20). 13 Steps to Take to Achieve Your Goals This Year. *WhoWhatWear.* https://thethirty.whowhatwear.com/how-to-set-realistic-expectations/slide19

Yoast, M. (2016, April 14). Designing an ecosystem for academic excellence: 7 elements to consider. *Renaissance.* https://www.renaissance.com/2016/

04/14/designing-an-ecosystem-for-excellence-7-elements/

———————

Uncredited Web Articles

AdventHealth. (2019, October 8.). 5 Signs You Should Talk to Your Doctor About Anxiety. *Advent Health.* https://www.adventhealth.com/hospital/adventhealth-orlando/blog/5-signs-you-should-talk-your-doctor-about-anxiety

American Heart Association Editorial Staff. (n.d.). Understanding How Stress Affects the Body. *American Heart Association.* https://www.heart.org/en/healthy-living/healthy-lifestyle/stress-management/lower-stress-how-does-stress-affect-the-body

Comedy therapy: Coping with anxiety one laugh at a time. (n.d.). *Anxiety.org.* https://www.anxiety.org/comedy-therapy-coping-with-anxiety-one-laugh-at-a-time

Factorial HR. (2022, July 26). What is a growth mindset and how to encourage it at work. *Factorial.* https://factorialhr.com/blog/growth-mindset-meaning/#:~:text=The%20growth%20mindset%20meaning%20is,out%20inspiration%20in%20others'%20success.

HBR Editors. (2014, November). How Companies Can Profit from a "Growth Mindset." *Harvard Business Review.* https://hbr.org/2014/11/how-companies-can-profit-from-a-growth-mindset

How do I set realistic expectations? (2020, July 20). *Valiant Living.* https://www.valiantdetox.com/how-do-i-set-realistic-expectations/

How to Build a Support System. (2022, December 16). *7 Summit Pathways.* https://7summitpathways.com/blog/how-to-build-a-support-system

Indeed Editorial Team. (2022, June 24). Top 15 Traits of Successful People. *Indeed.* https://www.indeed.com/career-advice/career-development/trait-of-successful-people

Mayo Clinic Staff. (2023, September 22). Stress relief from laughter? It's no joke. When it comes to relieving stress, more giggles and guffaws are just what the doctor ordered. Here's why. *Mayo Clinic* https://www.mayoclinic.org/healthy-lifestyle/stress-management/in-depth/stress-relief/art-20044456

Mental Health First Aid USA. (2020, August 6). The Importance of Having a Support System. *Mental Health First Aid.* https://www.mentalhealthfirstaid.org/2020/08/the-importance-of-having-a-support-system/

Other News (22 Nov. 2000). Laughter is indeed the best medicine. *Farm and*

Dairy. https://www.farmanddairy.com/news/laughter-is-indeed-the-best-medicine/3707.html

Physical activity and mental health. (n.d.). *Mental Health Foundation.* https://www.mentalhealth.org.uk/explore-mental-health/a-z-topics/physical-activity-and-mental-health#:~:text=Physical%20activi-ty%20is%20not%20only,us%20can%20do%20for%20free!

Timely Team. (2023, June 7). How to set realistic goals. *Timely.* https://timelyapp.com/blog/how-to-set-realistic-goals

Top 10 Panic Attack Triggers. (2021, February 3). *Banyan Mental Health.* https://www.banyanmentalhealth.com/2021/02/03/top-10-panic-attack-triggers/

What is overthinking and what can we do about it? (2022, August 17). *Great Minds Clinic Blog.* https://www.greatmindsclinic.co.uk/blog/what-is-overthinking-and-what-can-we-do-about-it/

When Do Anxiety and Depression Require Professional Help? (n.d.). *River City Family Medicine.* https://www.rivercityfamilymedicine.com/blog/when-do-anxiety-and-depression-require-professional-help

When Does Anxiety Warrant Professional Help? (n.d.). *Plymouth Psych Group.* https://www.plymouthpsychgroup.com/blog/when-does-anxiety-warrant-professional-help

5 Mental Benefits of Exercise. (n.d.). *Walden University.* https://www.waldenu.edu/online-bachelors-programs/bs-in-psychology/resource/five-mental-benefits-of-exercise

5 Traits of a Healthy Support System. (n.d.). *Vantage Point.* https://vantage pointrecovery.com/healthy-support-system/

200 Best Comedy Series of All Time. (n.d.). *Rotten Tomatoes.* https://editorial.rottentomatoes.com/guide/best-comedy-shows-of-all-time/

FAMOUS QUOTES

Angelou, Maya. Success is liking yourself, liking what you do, and liking how you do it. *System 4 Utah.* https://system4utah.com/2017/11/20/success-is-liking-yourself-liking-what-you-do-and-liking-how-you-do-it-maya-angelou/

Einstein, Albert: In every difficulty lies opportunity. *Quotesberry.* https://quotesberry.com/albert-einstein-in-the-middle-of-every-difficulty-lies-opportunity/

Rivers, Joan. The first time I see a jogger smiling, I'll consider it. *The Swiss Quality Consulting: Digital Transformation Services.* https://theswissquality. ch/the-first-time-i-see-a-jogger-smiling-ill-consider-it-joa/

Twain, Mark. When we remember we are all mad, the mysteries disappear and life stands explained. *Good Reads.* https://www.goodreads.com/ quotes/21938-when-we-remember-we-are-all-mad-the-mysteries-disap pear

SARA TONINSTAN ON SOCIAL MEDIA

If you're not already part of my punk circus over on Instagram, I encourage to join the party now! You can also find me on Facebook and TikTok. Embrace your quirks & manage the chaos.

SARCRASSTIC.SELF.CARE ON INSTAGRAM

Sarcrasstic.Self.Care ON FACEBOOK

Sarcrasstic.Self.Care ON TikTOK

Chez Sarcrasstic Self Care:

- Freak Flags Fly High
- Kindness is Key
- Laughter is Abundant
- Punk Attitude Prevails
- ADHD Rebels Find Their Groove.

I talk a lot about ADHD, rant about the patriarchy, and even throw menopause into the mix. BUT:

- You don't have to have ADHD to be included & find friends + a safe home here.
- You don't have to be a woman.
- You don't have to be a Gen Xer or even an Elder Millennial to rave at this club.

This is an all ages, gender-inclusive, anti-racist space where we take livin', laughin' & lovin' to the next fvckin' level. Ok? War babies, Boomers, Gen Xers, Millennials & Zoomers, I love you all. Now, share this with someone who needs to hear it to spread intergenerational love & appreciation.

You're a badass.
You know that, right?

ABOUT THE AUTHOR

Sara Toninstan is a pen name (and a pun: Serotonin Stan, get it?). Her alter ego and the real brains of this operation, Sarah Glasco, is a late-diagnosed ADHD writer, former tenured college professor & published scholar, multi-instrumentalist rock musician, and mom to two full-grown neurodivergent kids.

A classically trained cellist, fluent French speaker with a Ph.D., and once a manager of the Wine & Cheese Department at a Whole Foods Market in her mid-twenties, Sara(h) would have made an exquisite wealthy elitist snob. (Un)fortunately, however, she has a knack for chasing passions that never really pay that well. Her current hyper-fixations include ADHD & menopause, her own happiness & well-being, her dog, and living life on her own bullsh*t-free terms.

Sara(h) resides in Hillsborough, North Carolina (USA) with her awesomely kooky partner and adorable pit bull mix dog, Kubo.

Printed in Great Britain
by Amazon